Henry Morley, George Peele

Plays and Poems by George Peele

Henry Morley, George Peele

Plays and Poems by George Peele

ISBN/EAN: 9783744714129

Printed in Europe, USA, Canada, Australia, Japan

Cover: Foto ©Thomas Meinert / pixelio.de

More available books at **www.hansebooks.com**

BY

GEORGE PEELE

WITH AN INTRODUCTION BY HENRY MORLEY
LL.D., PROFESSOR OF ENGLISH LITERATURE AT
UNIVERSITY COLLEGE, LONDON

.

LONDON
GEORGE ROUTLEDGE AND SONS
BROADWAY, LUDGATE HILL
GLASGOW AND NEW YORK
1887

MORLEY'S UNIVERSAL LIBRARY.

" Marvels of clear type and general neatness."—*Daily Telegraph.*

INTRODUCTION.

GEORGE PEELE was born in the year of Queen Elizabeth's accession to the throne.

From a MS. volume of Depositions in the University Court at Oxford, Dr. Bliss found that, in a question of property, George Peele was examined on the 29th of March 1583, on the part of John Yate. Before his deposition, Peele is described as of the City of London, gentleman; resident in London for nearly two years; and, before that, for nine years in the University of Oxford. He is said also to be a deponent twenty-five years old. This gives 1558 for the year of his birth, and 1581, a little later than the end of March, for the time of his leaving Oxford.

Antony à Wood says, in the *Athenæ Oxonienses*, that he was of a Devonshire family; that "he was first sent to Broadgates Hall" (now Pembroke College), "was after some time made Student of Christ Church, 1573 or thereabouts, where, going through the several forms of Logic and Philosophy, he took the degrees in Arts, that of Master being completed in 1579, at which time he was esteemed a most noted poet in the University." This would make Peele a Master of Arts at Christ Church in 1579, at the age of twenty-one. In that year Edmund Spenser, who was about five years older, first made his mark as a poet, by the publication of his "Shepherd's Calendar." Peele having remained at Oxford for another two years, with reputation of a poet, left in the spring of 1583 to seek his fortune in London. In the following year, 1584 —which was two years before Shakespeare came to London, and eight years before Shakespeare began to produce his own creations—Peele's graceful Court play, "The Arraignment of Paris," was produced before Elizabeth by the Children of her Chapel, and in the same year it was printed. Three years afterwards Thomas Nash wrote of Peele in an Address to the Gentlemen Students of both Universities, " I dare commend him unto all that know him as the chief supporter of pleasaunce now living, the Atlas of poetry, and *primum verborum Artifex:* whose first increase, 'The Arraignment of Paris,' might plead to your opinions his present dexterity of wit and manifold variety of invention, wherein (*me judice*) he goeth a step beyond all that write." And certainly there is a dainty grace in the plan and execution of that play written to please and compliment the Queen. It gave first earnest of the new wealth of poetry that our dramatists only two or three years afterwards would begin to pour into our Literature. There is still the early use of rhyme; the only blank verse in the play being the oration of Paris before the gods. It was not until Marlowe began his career with "Tamburlaine," two or three years later than Peele's "Arraignment of Paris," that reaction against the "jigging vein of rhyming mother wits" began. It is interesting also to notice in this play one evidence of the high estimation in which Spenser's "Shepherd's Calendar" was held, Peele's shepherd interlude in the third act, preluding the lament of Œnone, being inspired wholly by that poem, and adopting from it names of characters.

It was about 1586, the year in which Shakespeare, aged twenty-two, is supposed to have first come to London, that the six or seven years of a new vigour on the English stage began, and Marlowe, Peele, Greene, Lodge, and others represented the first ripe fruits of the tree which had been planted five-and-twenty years before, and had been vigorously growing with production of much blossom and leaf. Peele continued to write, and lived as a poet and dramatist among the comrades of his craft, shared with them the temptations to excess incident to a time when much of social life was in the taverns, where the wits sat shoulder to shoulder with the drunkards and with men whose lives were low. How far Peele was dragged down it is difficult to know. He must have married within two years of his first coming to

London, for his Deposition at Oxford was occasioned by his wife's interest in the matter in question. His poem, written in 1593, to celebrate the installation of five Knights of the Garter; his stirring Farewell to Drake and Norris, in 1589; his poem, in 1589, on the return of Essex from Portugal; his celebrations of the completion of the thirty-second and thirty-seventh years of the Queen's Reign on the 17th of November 1590 and 1595 ("Polyhymnia" and "Anglorum Feriæ"); seem to indicate relations of the poet with the Court and with the nobles of the Court.

But in January 1596, George Peele, in sickness and poverty, sent to Lord Burleigh, then High Treasurer of England, this note with a revised reprint of his early poem, " A Tale of Troy," written in early college days, first printed in 1589, and bearing marks of immaturity :

> Salve Parens Patriæ, tibi plebs, tibi curia nomen
> Hoc dedit, hoc dedimus nos tibi nomen, eques.
> [Parent of Fatherland, hail, so Court and Country declare you,
> And to you I, O Knight, also attribute the name.]

" In these terms, right honourable, am I bold to salute your Lordship, whose high deserts in our England's great designs have earned large praises even from Envy's mouth. Pardon, great patron of learning and virtue, this rude encounter, in that I presume—a scholar of so mean merit—to present your wisdom with this small manual, by this simple messenger, my eldest daughter, and Necessity's servant. Long sickness having so enfeebled me maketh bashfulness almost become impudency. Sed quis psittaco suum χαίρε expedivit? Magister artis, ingeniique largitor, venter.* The subject wherewith I presume to greet your honour, is the History of Troy, in 500 verses set down, and memorable accidents thereof. Receive it, noble Senator of England's Council-house, as a scholar's duty's signification, and live long in honour and prosperity, as happy as Queen Elizabeth's gracious countenance can make you.

---

* From the Prologue to the Satires of Persius :
> " Who taught the parrot human notes to try,
> Or with a voice endued the chattering pie ?
> Twas witty want, fierce hunger to appease :
> Want taught their masters, and their masters these."
> DRYDEN'S *Translation.*

" Ecce tibi nihilum magno pro munere mitto ;
Esse potest aliquid, te capiente, nihil.
[See, for a large gift here what I send you is but a Nothing ;
When it is you who receive, Nothing to Something can turn.]

" Your Honour's most bounden

" GEORGE PEELE."

In 1598 George Peele is, by Francis Meres, in his " Palladis Tamia," spoken of as dead.

In the poem on the Order of the Garter, Peele had written :

' I laid me down, laden with many cares,
My bedfellows almost these twenty years ; "

and in the Introduction to that poem the reader will observe a pathetic reference to Marlowe, who had been killed in a tavern brawl only a few weeks before those lines were written.

In " The Old Wives' Tale " there is a playful grace that would make the piece a pleasant one to act before an audience of children ; though they would know little of the good-humoured banter of the brother poets who did battle for English hexameters, in Huanebango's " sulphurous huff snuff," and would trouble themselves little with question about the relations of Sacrapant and Delia and her two brothers to Comus and the Lady in Comus.

" David and Bethsabe," which Mr. Dyce considered to be Peele's masterpiece, is a Scriptural play shaped out of the Second Book of Samuel, being a dramatic paraphrase of the eleventh and next following chapters as far as the eighth verse of the nineteenth. I have ventured in this volume to supply the division into Acts and Scenes, which had not been indicated in the printed copies.

There are other works of George Peele which are not included in this volume, but with the exception of one work, which is given in another volume of this Library, here are the writings by which Peele lives and will live.

H. M.

July 1887.

CONTENTS.

PLAYS.

POEMS.

THE ARRAIGNMENT OF PARIS.

A.D. 1584 — See p. 6.

DRAMATIS PERSONÆ.

SATURN.	SILVANUS.	FLORA.
JUPITER.	PARIS.	RHANIS.
NEPTUNE.	COLIN.	ATE.
PLUTO.	HOBBINOL.	CLOTHO.
APOLLO.	DIGGON.	LACHESIS.
MARS.	THENOT.	ATROPOS.
BACCHUS.	JUNO.	THE MUSES.
MERCURY.	PALLAS.	A NYMPH OF DIANA.
VULCAN.	VENUS.	ŒNONE.
PAN.	DIANA.	HELEN.
FAUNUS.	POMONA.	THESTYLIS.

Cupids, Cyclops, Shepherds, Knights, &c.

Enter ATE, *Prologus.*

CONDEMNÉD soul, Até, from lowest hell,
And deadly rivers of th' infernal Jove,
Where bloodless ghosts in pains of endless date
Fill ruthless ears with never-ceasing cries,
Behold, I come in place, and bring beside
The bane of Troy! Behold, the fatal fruit,

Raught from the golden tree of Proserpine!
Proud Troy must fall, so bid the gods above,
And stately Ilium's lofty towers be razed
By conquering hands of the victorious foe ;
King Priam's palace waste with flaming fire,
Whose thick and foggy smoke, piercing the sky,
Must serve for messenger of sacrifice
T' appease the anger of the angry heavens ;
And Priam's younger son, the shepherd swain,
Paris, th' unhappy organ of the Greeks.
So loth and weary of her heavy load,
The Earth complains unto the hellish prince,
Surcharged with the burden that she nill sustain ;
Th' unpartial daughters of Necessity
Bin aiders in her suit : and so the twine
That holds old Priam's house, the thread of Troy,
Dame Atropos with knife in sunder cuts.
Done be the pleasure of the powers above,
Whose hests men must obey : and I my part
Perform in Ida vales.   Lordings, adieu ;
Imposing silence for your task, I end,
Till just assembly of the goddesses
Make me begin the tragedy of Troy.

                    [*Exit cum aureo pomo.*

ACT I.

SCENE I.

Enter PAN, FAUNUS, *and* SILVANUS, *with their*
ATTENDANTS, *to give welcome to the goddesses :*
PAN'S SHEPHERD *has a lamb,* FAUNUS' HUNTER
has a fawn, SILVANUS' WOODMAN *with an oaken-
bough laden with acorns.*

PAN. Silvanus, either Flora doth us wrong
Or Faunus made us tarry all too long,   ;
For by this morning mirth it should appear,
The Muses or the Goddesses be near.
    FAUN. My fawn was nimble, Pan, and whipt
      apace—
'Twas happy that we caught him up at last—
The fattest, fairest fawn in all the chase ;
    I wonder how the knave could skip so fast.
    PAN. And I have brought a twagger for the
      nones,
A bunting lamb ; nay, pray you feel no bones :
Believe me now my cunning much I miss,
If ever Pan felt fatter lamb than this.
    SIL. Sirs, you may boast your flocks and herds
      that bin both fresh and fair,

Yet hath Silvanus walks, i-wis, that stand in whole-
　　some air ;
And, lo, the honour of the woods, the gallant oaken-
　　bough,
Do I bestow, laden with acorns and with mast
　　enow !
　　PAN. Peace, man, for shame ! shalt have both
　　　　lambs and dams and flocks and herds and all,
And all my pipes to make thee glee ; we meet not
　　now to brawl.
　　FAUN. There's no such matter, Pan ; we are all
　　　　friends assembled hither,
To bid Queen Juno and her feres most humbly
　　welcome hither :
Diana, mistress of our woods, her presence will not
　　want ;
Her courtesy to all her friends, we wot, is nothing
　　scant.

Enter POMONA *with her fruit.*

　　POM. Yea, Pan, no farther yet, and had the start
　　　　of me ?
Why, then, Pomona with her fruit comes time
　　enough, I see.
Come on a while ; with country store, like friends,
　　we venture forth :

Think'st, Faunus, that these goddesses will take our
    gifts in worth ?

    FAUN. Yea, doubtless, for shall tell thee, dame,
    'twere better give a thing,

A sign of love, unto a mighty person or a king,

Than to a rude and barbarous swain, but bad and
    basely born,

For gently takes the gentleman that oft the clown
    will scorn.

    PAN. Say'st truly, Faunus; I myself have given
    good tidy lambs

To Mercury, may say to thee, to Phœbus, and to
    Jove ;

When to a country mops, forsooth, chave offered all
    their dams,

And piped and prayed for little worth, and ranged
    about the grove.

    POM. God Pan, that makes your flock so thin,
    and makes you look so lean,

To kiss in corners.

    PAN.   Well said, wench! some other
    thing you mean.

    POM. Yea, jest it out till it go alone ; but marvel
    where we miss

Fair Flora all this merry morn.

    FAUN.   Some news ; see where she is.

Enter FLORA.

PAN. Flora, well met, and for thy taken pain,
Poor country gods, thy debtors we remain.

    FLO. Believe me, Pan, not all thy lambs and
        ewes,
Nor, Faunus, all thy lusty bucks and does,
(But that I am instructed well to know
What service to the hills and dales I owe,)
Could have enforced me to so strange a toil,
Thus to enrich this gaudy, gallant soil.

    FAUN. But tell me, wench, hast done't so trick
        indeed,
That heaven itself may wonder at the deed?

    FLO. Not Iris, in her pride and bravery,
Adorns her arch with such variety;
Nor doth the milk-white way, in frosty night,
Appear so fair and beautiful in sight,
As don these fields, and groves, and sweetest
        bowers,
Bestrewed and decked with parti-coloured flowers.
Along the bubbling brooks and silver glide
That at the bottom do in silence slide,
The water-flowers and lilies on the banks,
Like blazing comets, burgeon all in ranks;
Under the hawthorn and the poplar-tree,
Where sacred Phœbe may delight to be,

The primrose, and the purple hyacinth,
The dainty violet, and the wholesome minth,
The double daisy, and the cowslip, queen
Of summer flowers, do overpeer the green ;
And round about the valley as ye pass,
Ye may ne see for peeping flowers the grass :
That well the mighty Juno, and the rest,
May boldly think to be a welcome guest
On Ida hills, when to approve the thing,
The Queen of Flowers prepares a second spring.

    SIL. Thou gentle nymph, what thanks shall we
       repay
To thee that mak'st our fields and woods so gay ?

    FLO. Silvanus, when it is thy hap to see
My workmanship in portraying all the three,
First stately Juno with her port and grace,
Her robes, her lawns, her crownet, and her mace,
Would make thee muse this picture to behold,
Of yellow oxlips bright as burnished gold.

    POM. A rare device ; and Flora well, perdy,
Did paint her yellow for her jealousy.

    FLO. Pallas in flowers of hue and colours red ;
Her plumes, her helm, her lance, her Gorgon's head,
Her trailing tresses that hang flaring round,
Of July-flowers so graffèd in the ground,
That, trust me, sirs, who did the cunning see,
Would at a blush suppose it to be she.

PAN. Good Flora, by my flock, 'twere very good
To dight her all in red resembling blood.

FLO. Fair Venus of sweet violets in blue,
With other flowers infixed for change of hue;
Her plumes, her pendants, bracelets, and her
    rings,
Her dainty fan, and twenty other things,
Her lusty mantle waving in the wind,
And every part in colour and in kind;
And for her wreath of roses, she nill dare
With Flora's cunning counterfeit compare.
So that what living wight shall chance to see
These goddesses, each placed in her degree,
Portrayed by Flora's workmanship alone,
Must say that art and nature met in one.

SIL. A dainty draught to lay her down in blue,
The colour commonly betokening true.

FLO. This piece of work, compact with many a
    flower,
And well laid in at entrance of the bower,
Where Phœbe means to make this meeting royal,
Have I prepared to welcome them withal.

POM. And are they yet dismounted, Flora, say,
That we may wend to meet them on the way?

FLO. That shall not need: they are at hand by
    this,
And the conductor of the train hight Rhanis.

Juno hath left her chariot long ago,
And hath returned her peacocks by her rainbow ;
And bravely, as becomes the wife of Jove,
Doth honour by her presence to our grove.
Fair Venus she hath let her sparrows fly,
To tend on her and make her melody ;
Her turtles and her swans unyokéd be,
And flicker near her side for company.
Pallas hath set her tigers loose to feed,
Commanding them to wait when she hath need.
And hitherward with proud and stately pace,
To do us honour in the sylvan chase,
They march, like to the pomp of heaven above,
Juno the wife and sister of King Jove,
The warlike Pallas, and the Queen of Love.

    PAN. Pipe, Pan, for joy, and let thy shepherds
       sing ;
Shall never age forget this memorable thing.

    FLO. Clio, the sagest of the Sisters Nine,
To do observance to this dame divine,
Lady of learning and of chivalry,
Is here arrivéd in fair ássembly ;
And wandering up and down th' unbeaten ways,
Ring through the wood sweet songs of Pallas' praise.

    POM. Hark, Flora, Faunus! here is melody,
A charm of birds, and more than ordinary.

        [An artificial charm of birds heard within.

PAN. The silly birds make mirth ; then should we do them wrong,
Pomona, if we nill bestow an echo to their song.

THE SONG.

[A choir within and without.]

GODS. O Ida, O Ida, O Ida, happy hill !
This honour done to Ida may it continue still !
    MUSES [*within*]. Ye country gods that in this Ida wone,
Bring down your gifts of welcome,
    For honour done to Ida.
    GODS. Behold, in sign of joy we sing,
And signs of joyful welcome bring,
    For honour done to Ida.
    MUSES [*within*]. The Muses give you melody to gratulate this chance,
And Phœbe, chief of sylvan chace, commands you all to dance.
    GODS. Then round in a circle our sportance must be ;
Hold hands in a hornpipe, all gallant in glee.

                             [Dance.

    MUSES [*within*]. Reverence, reverence, most humble reverence !
    GODS. Most humble reverence !

RHANIS *leading the way, enter* JUNO, PALLAS, *and* VENUS. PAN *alone sings.*

THE SONG.

The God of shepherds, and his mates,
    With country cheer salute your states,
Fair, wise, and worthy as you be,
    And thank the gracious ladies three
        For honour done to Ida.   [*The birds sing.*

JUNO. Venus, what shall I say? for, though I be
    a dame divine,
This welcome and this melody exceed these wits of
    mine.
    VEN. Believe me, Juno, as I hight the Sovereign
    of Love,
These rare delights in pleasure pass the banquets of
    King Jove.
    PAL. Then, Venus, I conclude, it easily may be
    seen,
That in her chaste and pleasant walks fair Phœbe is
    a queen.
    RHA. Divine Pallas, and you, O sacred dames,
Juno and Venus, honoured by your names,
Juno, the wife and sister of King Jove,
Fair Venus, lady-president of love,

If any entertainment in this place,
That can afford but homely, rude, and base,
It please your godheads to accept in gree,
That gracious thought our happiness shall be.
My mistress Dian, this right well I know,
For love that to this presence she doth owe,
Accounts more honour done to her this day,
Than ever whilom in these woods of Ida;
And for our country gods, I dare be bold,
They make such cheer, your presence to behold,
Such jouissance, such mirth, and merriment,
As nothing else their mind might more content:
And that you do believe it to be so,
Fair goddesses, your lovely looks do show. .
It rests in fine, for to confirm my talk,
Ye deign to pass along to Dian's walk;
Where she among her troop of maids attends
The fair arrival of her welcome friends.

    FLO. And we will wait with all observance
      due,
And do just honour to this heavenly crew.

    PAN. The God of Shepherds, Juno, ere thou go,
Intends a lamb on thee for to bestow.

    FAUN. Faunus, high ranger in Diana's chase,
Presents a fawn to Lady Venus' grace.

    SIL. Silvanus gives to Pallas' deity
This gallant bough raught from the oaken-tree.

POM. To them that do this honour to our fields
Her mellow apples poor Pomona yields.

JUNO. And, gentle gods, these signs of your
goodwill
We take in worth, and shall accept them still.

VEN. And, Flora, this to thee among the
rest—
Thy workmanship comparing with the best,
Let it suffice thy cunning to have power
To call King Jove from forth his heavenly bower.
Hadst thou a lover, Flora, credit me,
I think thou wouldst bedeck him gallantly.
But wend we on ; and, Rhanis, lead the way,
That kens the painted paths of pleasant Ida.

[*Exeunt.*

SCENE II.

Enter PARIS *and* ŒNONE.

PAR. Œnone, while we bin disposed to walk,
Tell me what shall be subject of our talk ?
Thou hast a sort of pretty tales in store,
Dare say no nymph in Ida woods hath more :
Again, beside thy sweet alluring face,
In telling them thou hast a special grace.
Then, prithee, sweet, afford some pretty thing,
Some toy that from thy pleasant wit doth spring.

ŒN. Paris, my heart's contentment and my
    choice,
Use thou thy pipe, and I will use my voice ;
So shall thy just request not be denied,
And time well spent, and both be satisfied.
    PAR. Well, gentle nymph, although thou do me
    wrong,
That can ne tune my pipe unto a song,
Me list this once, Œnone, for thy sake,
This idle task on me to undertake.
                  [*They sit under a tree together.*
    ŒN. And whereon, then, shall be my roundelay ?
For thou hast heard my store long since, dare say ;
How Saturn did divide his kingdom tho
To Jove, to Neptune, and to Dis below ;
How mighty men made foul successless war
Against the gods and state of Jupiter ;
How Phorcys' imp, that was so trick and fair,
That tangled Neptune in her golden hair,
Became a Gorgon for her lewd misdeed,—
A pretty fable, Paris, for to read,
A piece of cunning, trust me, for the nones,
That wealth and beauty alter men to stones ;
How Salmacis, resembling idleness,
Turns men to women all through wantonness ;
How Pluto raught Queen Ceres' daughter thence
And what did follow of that love-offence ;

Of Daphne turned into the laurel-tree,
That shows a mirror of virginity ;
How fair Narcissus tooting on his shade,
Reproves disdain, and tells how form doth vade ;
How cunning Philomela's needle tells
What force in love, what wit in sorrow dwells ;
What pains unhappy souls abide in hell,
They say, because on earth they lived not well,—
Ixion's wheel, proud Tantal's pining woe,
Prometheus' torment, and a many mo,
How Danaus' daughters ply their endless task,
What toil the toil of Sisyphus doth ask :
All these are old and known I know, yet, if thou
    wilt have any,
Choose some of these, for, trust me, else Œnone hath
    not many.
    PAR. Nay, what thou wilt : but sith my cunning
    not compares with thine,
Begin some toy that I can play upon this pipe of
    mine.
    ŒN. There is a pretty sonnet, then, we call it
    " Cupid's Curse,"
" They that do change old love for new, pray gods
    they change for worse ! "
The note is fine and quick withal, the ditty will agree,
Paris, with that same vow of thine upon our poplar-
    tree.

PAR. No better thing; begin it, then; Œnone,
thou shalt see

Our music figure of the love that grows 'twixt thee
and me.

[*They sing; and while* ŒNONE *sings, he pipes.*

CUPID'S CURSE.

ŒN. Fair and fair, and twice so fair,
    As fair as any may be;
  The fairest shepherd on our green,
    A love for any lady.
PAR. Fair and fair, and twice so fair,
    As fair as any may be;
  Thy love is fair for thee alone,
    And for no other lady.
ŒN. My love is fair, my love is gay,
    As fresh as bin the flowers in May,
  And of my love my roundelay,
    My merry merry merry roundelay,
    Concludes with Cupid's curse,—
  They that do change old love for new,
    Pray gods they change for worse!
BOTH. They that do change, &c.
ŒN. Fair and fair, &c.
PAR. Fair and fair, &c.
  Thy love is fair, &c.

ŒN. My love can pipe, my love can sing,
   My love can many a pretty thing,
   And of his lovely praises ring
   My merry merry roundelays,
     Amen to Cupid's curse,—
   They that do change, &c.
PAR. They that do change, &c.
BOTH. Fair and fair, &c.

          [*The song being ended, they rise.*

ŒN. Sweet shepherd, for Œnone's sake be cunning in this song,
And keep thy love, and love thy choice, or else thou dost her wrong.
   PAR. My vow is made and witnessèd, the poplar will not start,
Nor shall the nymph Œnone's love from forth my breathing heart.
I will go bring thee on thy way, my flock are here behind,
And I will have a lover's fee ; they say, unkissed, unkind.   [*Exeunt.*

ACT II.

SCENE I.

Enter JUNO, PALLAS, *and* VENUS.

VEN. [*ex abrupto*]. But pray you, tell me, Juno,
  was it so,
As Pallas told me here the tale of Echo?
  JUNO. She was a nymph indeed, as Pallas tells,
A walker, such as in these thickets dwells ;
And as she told what subtle juggling pranks
She played with Juno, so she told her thanks :
A tattling trull to come at every call,
And now, forsooth, nor tongue nor life at all.
And though perhaps she was a help to Jove,
And held me chat while he might court his love,
Believe me, dames, I am of this opinion,
He took but little pleasure in the minion ;
And whatsoe'er his scapes have been beside,
Dare say for him, 'a never strayed so wide :
A lovely nut-brown lass or lusty trull
Have power perhaps to make a god a bull.
  VEN. Gramercy, gentle Juno, for that jest ;
I'faith, that item was worth all the rest.
  PAL. No matter, Venus, howsoe'er you scorn,
My father Jove at that time ware the horn.

JUNO. Had every wanton god above, Venus, not better luck,

Then heaven would be a pleasant park, and Mars a lusty buck.

VEN. Tut, Mars hath horns to butt withal, although no bull 'a shows,

'A never needs to mask in nets, 'a fears no jealous froes.

JUNO. Forsooth, the better is his turn, for, if 'a speak too loud,

Must find some shift to shadow him, a net or else a cloud.

PAL. No more of this, fair goddesses ; unrip not so your shames,

To stand all naked to the world, that bene such heavenly dames.

JUNO. Nay, Pallas, that's a common trick with Venus well we know,

And all the gods in heaven have seen her naked long ago.

VEN. And then she was so fair and bright, so lovely and so trim,

As Mars is but for Venus' tooth, and she will sport with him :

And, but me list not here to make comparison with Jove,

Mars is no ranger, Juno, he, in every open grove.

PAL. Too much of this : we wander far, the skies
    begin to scowl ;
Retire we to Diana's bower, the weather will be
    foul.

> [*The storm being past of thunder and light-*
> *ning, and* ATE *having trundled the ball*
> *into place, crying,* "*Fatum Trojæ,*" JUNO
> *takes it up.*

JUNO. Pallas, the storm is past and gone, and
    Phœbus clears the skies,
And, lo, behold a ball of gold, a fair and worthy
    prize !
    VEN. This posy wills the apple to the fairest given
    be ;
Then is it mine, for Venus hight the fairest of the
    three.
    PAL. The fairest here, as fair is meant, am I, ye
    do me wrong ;
And if the fairest have it must, to me it doth belong.
    JUNO. Then Juno may it not enjoy, so every one
    says no,
But I will prove myself the fairest, ere I lose it so.

> [*They read the posy.*

The brief is this, *Detur pulcherrimæ,*
Let this unto the fairest given be,
The fairest of the three,—and I am she.
    PAL. *Detur pulcherrimæ,*

Let this unto the fairest given be,
The fairest of the three,—and I am she.

VEN. *Detur pulcherrimæ,*
Let this unto the fairest given be,
The fairest of the three,—and I am she.

JUNO. My face is fair; but yet the majesty,
That all the gods in heaven have seen in me,
Have made them choose me, of the planets seven,
To be the wife of Jove and queen of heaven.
If, then, this prize be but bequeathed to beauty,
The only she that wins this prize am I.

VEN. That Venus is the fairest, this doth prove,
That Venus is the lovely Queen of Love:
The name of Venus is indeed but beauty,
And men me fairest call per excellency.
If, then, this prize be but bequeathed to beauty,
The only she that wins this prize am I.

PAL. To stand on terms of beauty as you take it,
Believe me, ladies, is but to mistake it.
The beauty that this subtle prize must win,
No outward beauty hight, but dwells within ;
And sift it as you please, and you shall find,
This beauty is the beauty of the mind :
This fairness, virtue hight in general,
That many branches hath in special ⊱
This beauty wisdom hight, whereof am I,
By heaven appointed, goddess worthily.

And look how much the mind, the better part,
Doth overpass the body in desert,
So much the mistress of those gifts divine
Excels thy beauty, and that state of thine.
Then, if this prize be thus bequeathed to beauty,
The only she that wins this prize am I.

VEN. Nay, Pallas, by your leave you wander
  clean :
We must not construe hereof as you mean,
But take the sense as it is plainly meant ;
And let the fairest ha't, I am content.

PAL. Our reasons will be infinite, I trow,
Unless unto some other point we grow :
But first here's none, methinks, disposed to yield,
And none but will with words maintain the field.

JUNO. Then, if you will, t' avoid a tedious grudge,
Refer it to the sentence of a judge ;
Whoe'er he be that cometh next in place,
Let him bestow the ball and end the case.

VEN. So can it not go wrong with me at all.

PAL. I am agreed, however it befall :
And yet by common doom, so may it be,
I may be said the fairest of the three.

JUNO. Then yonder, lo, that shepherd swain is
  he,
That must be umpire in this controversy !

Enter PARIS.

VEN. Juno, in happy time, I do accept the man ;
It seemeth by his looks some skill of love he can.

PAR. [*aside*]. The nymph is gone, and I, all
solitary,
Must wend to tend my charge, oppressed with
melancholy.
This day (or else me fails my shepherd's skill)
Will tide me passing good or passing ill.

JUNO. Shepherd, abash not, though at sudden
thus
Thou be arrived by ignorance among us,
Not earthly but divine, and goddesses all three ;
Juno, Pallas, Venus, these our titles be.
Nor fear to speak for reverence of the place,
Chosen to end a hard and doubtful case.
This apple, lo, (nor ask thou whence it came,)
Is to be given unto the fairest dame !
And fairest is, nor she, nor she, but she
Whom, shepherd, thou shalt fairest name to be.
This is thy charge ; fulfil without offence,
And she that wins shall give thee recompense.

PAL. Dread not to speak, for we have chosen thee
Sith in this case we can no judges be.

VEN. And, shepherd, say that I the fairest am,
And thou shalt win good guerdon for the same.

JUNO. Nay, shepherd, look upon my stately
grace,
Because the pomp that 'longs to Juno's mace
Thou mayst not see ; and think Queen Juno's
name,
To whom old shepherds title works of fame,
Is mighty, and may easily suffice,
At Phœbe's hand, to gain a golden prize.
And for thy meed, sith I am queen of riches,
Shepherd, I will reward thee with great monarchies,
Empires, and kingdoms, heaps of massy gold,
Sceptres and diadems curious to behold,
Rich robes, of sumptuous workmanship and cost,
And thousand things whereof I make no boast :
The mould whereon thou treadest shall be of Tagus'
sands,
And Xanthus shall run liquid gold for thee to wash
thy hands ;
And if thou like to tend thy flock, and not from
them to fly,
Their fleeces shall be curléd gold to please their
master's eye ;
And last, to set thy heart on fire, give this one fruit
to me,
And, shepherd, lo, this tree of gold will I bestow on
thee !

JUNO'S SHOW.

A Tree of Gold rises, laden with diadems and crowns
of gold.

The ground whereon it grows, the grass, the root of
    gold,
The body and the bark of gold, all glistering to
    behold,
The leaves of burnished gold, the fruits that thereon
    grow
Are diadems set with pearl in gold, in gorgeous
    glistering show ;
And if this tree of gold in lieu may not suffice,
Require a grove of golden trees, so Juno bear the
    prize.   [*The Tree sinks.*

    PAL. Me list not tempt thee with decaying wealth,
Which is embased by want of lusty health ;
But if thou have a mind to fly above,
Y-crowned with fame, near to the seat of Jove,
If thou aspire to wisdom's worthiness,
Whereof thou mayst not see the brightness,
If thou desire honour of chivalry,
To be renowned for happy victory,
To fight it out, and in the champaign field
To shroud thee under Pallas' warlike shield,

To prance on barbéd steeds, this honour, lo,
Myself for guerdon shall on thee bestow!
And for encouragement, that thou mayst see
What famous knights Dame Pallas' warriors be,
Behold in Pallas' honour here they come,
Marching along with sound of thundering drum.

PALLAS' SHOW.

Enter NINE KNIGHTS *in armour, treading a warlike
almain, by drum and fife ; and then they having
marched forth again,* VENUS *speaks.*

VEN. Come, shepherd, come, sweet shepherd, look
on me,
These bene too hot alarums, these, for thee :
But if thou wilt give me the golden ball,
Cupid my boy shall ha't to play withal,
That, whensoe'er this apple he shall see,
The God of Love himself shall think on thee,
And bid thee look and choose, and he will wound
Whereso thy fancy's object shall be found ;
And lightly when he shoots he doth not miss :
And I will give thee many a lovely kiss,
And come and play with thee on Ida here ;
And if thou wilt a face that hath no peer,
A gallant girl, a lusty minion lass,
That can give sport to thee thy thought to pass,

To ravish all thy beating veins with joy,
Here is a lass of Venus' court, my boy,
Here, gentle shepherd, here's for thee a piece,
The fairest face, the flower of gallant Greece.

VENUS' SHOW.

Enter HELEN *in her bravery, with four* CUPIDS
attending on her, each having his fan in his
hand to fan fresh air in her face : she sings as
follows :

    Se Diana nel cielo è una stella
    Chiara e lucente, piena di splendore,
    Che porge luc' all' affanato cuore ;

    Se Diana nel ferno è una dea
    Che da conforto all' anime dannate
    Che per amor son morte desperate ;

    Se Diana, ch' in terra è delle ninfe
    Reina imperativa di dolci fiori,
    Tra bosch' e selve da morte a pastori ;

    Io son un Diana dolce e rara,
    Che con li guardi io posso far guerra
    À Dian' infern', in cielo, e in terra.   [*Exit.*

PAR. Most heavenly dames, was never man as I,
Poor shepherd swain, so happy and unhappy ;
The least of these delights that you devise,
Able to rape and dazzle human eyes.

But since my silence may not pardoned be,
And I appoint which is the fairest she,
Pardon, most sacred dames, sith one, not all,
By Paris' doom must have this golden ball.
Thy beauty, stately Juno, dame divine,
That like to Phœbus' golden beams doth shine,
Approves itself to be most excellent ;
But that fair face that doth me most content,
Sith fair, fair dames, is neither she nor she,
But she whom I shall fairest deem to be,
That face is hers that hight the Queen of Love,
Whose sweetness doth both gods and creatures move ;
And if the fairest face deserve the ball,
Fair Venus, ladies, bears it from ye all.

              [Gives the golden ball to VENUS.

    VEN. And in this ball doth Venus more delight
Than in her lovely boy fair Cupid's sight.
Come, shepherd, come ; sweet Venus is thy friend ;
No matter how thou other gods offend.

            *[*VENUS *takes* PARIS *away with her.*

    JUNO. But he shall rue and ban the dismal day
Wherein his Venus bare the ball away ;
And heaven and earth just witnesses shall be,
I will revenge it on his progeny.

    PAL. Well, Juno, whether we be lief or loth,
Venus hath got the apple from us both.   *[Exeunt.*

A C T   I I I.

SCENE I.

Enter COLIN, *who sings his passion of love.*

O gentle Love, ungentle for thy deed,
    Thou mak'st my heart .
    A bloody mark
With piercing shot to bleed !
Shoot soft, sweet Love, for fear thou shoot amiss,
    For fear too keen
    Thy arrows bene,
And hit the heart where my belovéd is.
Too fair that fortune were, nor never I
    Shall be so blest,
    Among the rest,
That Love shall seize on her by sympathy.
Then since with Love my prayers bear no boot,
    This doth remain
    To ease my pain,
I take the wound, and die at Venus' foot.   [*Exit.*

Enter HOBBINOL, DIGGON, *and* THENOT.

HOB. Poor Colin, woful man, thy life forspoke
    by love,

What uncouth fit, what malady, is this that thou
dost prove ?

DIG. Or Love is void of physic clean, or Love's
our common wrack,

That gives us bane to bring us low, and lets us
medicine lack.

HOB. That ever Love had reverence 'mong silly
shepherd swains !

Belike that humour hurts them most that most might
be their pains.

THE. Hobbin, it is some other god that cherisheth
their sheep,

For sure this Love doth nothing else but make our
herdmen weep.

DIG. And what a hap is this, I pray, when all
our woods rejoice,

For Colin thus to be denied his young and lovely
choice ?

THE. She hight indeed so fresh and fair that well
it is for thee,

Colin, and kind hath been thy friend, that Cupid
could not see.

HOB. And whither wends yon thriveless swain ?
like to the stricken deer,   [here ?

Seeks he dictamnum for his wound within our forest

DIG. He wends to greet the Queen of Love, that
in these woods doth wone,

With mirthless lays to make complaint to Venus of
    her son.

    THE. Ah, Colin, thou art all deceived! she dallies
      with the boy,
And winks at all his wanton pranks, and thinks
    thy love a toy.

    HOB. Then leave him to his luckless love, let him
      abide his fate ;
The sore is rankled all too far, our comfort comes
    too late.

    DIG. Though Thestylis the scorpion be that breaks
      his sweet assault,
Yet will Rhamnusia vengeance take on her disdainful
    fault.

    THE. Lo, yonder comes the lovely nymph, that
      in these Ida vales   [dales !
Plays with Amyntas' lusty boy, and coys him in the

    HOB. Thenot, methinks her cheer is changed, her
      mirthful looks are laid,
She frolics not ; pray god, the lad have not beguiled
    the maid !

Enter ŒNONE *with a wreath of poplar on her head.*

    ŒN. [*aside*]. Beguiled, disdained, and out of love !
      Live long, thou poplar-tree,
And let thy letters grow in length, to witness this
    with me.

Ah, Venus, but for reverence unto thy sacred name.

To steal a silly maiden's love, I might account it blame!

And if the tales be true I hear, and blush for to recite,

Thou dost me wrong to leave the plains and dally out of sight.

False Paris, this was not thy vow, when thou and I were one,

To range and change old love for new ; but now those days be gone.

But I will find the goddess out, that she thy vow may read,

And fill these woods with my laments for thy unhappy deed.

  HOB. So fair a face, so foul a thought to harbour in his breast!

Thy hope consumed, poor nymph, thy hap is worse than all the rest.

  ŒN. Ah, shepherds, you bin full of wiles, and whet your wits on books,

And rape poor maids with pipes and songs, and sweet alluring looks!

  DIG. Mis-speak not all for his amiss ; there bin that keepen flocks,

That never chose but once, nor yet beguiléd love with mocks.

ŒN. False Paris, he is none of those ; his troth-
less double deed

Will hurt a many shepherds else that might go nigh
to speed.

THE. Poor Colin, that is ill for thee, that art as
true in trust

To thy sweet smart as to his nymph Paris hath been
unjust.

ŒN. Ah, well is she hath Colin won, that nill no
other love !

And woe is me, my luck is loss, my pains no pity
move !

HOB. Farewell, fair nymph, sith he must heal
alone that gave the wound ;

There grows no herb of such effect upon Dame
Nature's ground.

     [*Exeunt* HOBBINOL, DIGGON, *and* THENOT.

Enter MERCURY *with* VULCAN'S CYCLOPS.

MER. Here is a nymph that sadly sits, and she
beleek

Can tell some news, Pyracmon, of the jolly swain we
seek :

Dare wage my wings, the lass doth love, she looks
so bleak and thin ;

And 'tis for anger or for grief : but I will talk
begin.

ŒN. [*aside*]. Break out, poor heart, and make
    complaint, the mountain flocks to move,
What proud repulse and thankless scorn thou hast
    received of love.
MER. She singeth ; sirs, be hushed a while.
               [ŒNONE *sings as she sits.*

ŒNONE'S COMPLAINT.

Melpomene, the Muse of tragic songs,
With mournful tunes, in stole of dismal hue,
Assist a silly nymph to wail her woe,
And leave thy lusty company behind.

Thou luckless wreath ! becomes not me to wear
The poplar-tree for triumph of my love :
Then, as my joy, my pride of love, is left,
Be thou unclothéd of thy lovely green ;

And in thy leaves my fortune written be,
And them some gentle wind let blow abroad,
That all the world may see how false of love
False Paris hath to his Œnone been.
       [*The song ended,* ŒNONE *sitting still,*
         MERCURY *speaks.*
  MER. Good day, fair maid ; weary belike with
    following of your game,
I wish thee cunning at thy will, to spare or strike
    the same.

Œn. I thank you, sir ; my game is quick, and
 rids a length of ground,
And yet I am deceived, or else 'a had a deadly
 wound.
Mer. Your hand perhaps did swerve awry.
Œn.   Or else it was my heart.
Mer. Then sure 'a plied his footmanship.
Œn.   'A played a ranging part.
Mer. You should have given a deeper wound.
Œn.   I could not that for pity.
Mer. You should have eyed him better, then.
Œn.   Blind love was not so witty.
Mer. Why, tell me, sweet, are you in love ?
Œn.   Or would I were not so.
Mer. Ye mean because 'a does ye wrong.
Œn.   Perdy, the more my woe.
Mer. Why, mean ye Love, or him ye loved ?
Œn.   Well may I mean them both.
Mer. Is Love to blame ?
Œn.   The Queen of Love
      Hath made him false his troth.
Mer. Mean ye, indeed, the Queen of Love ?
Œn.   Even wanton Cupid's dame.
Mer. Why, was thy love so lovely, then ?
Œn.   His beauty hight his shame ;
The fairest shepherd on our green.
Mer.   Is he a shepherd, than ?

ŒN. And sometime kept a bleating flock.

MER.   Enough, this is the man.
Where wones he, then ?

ŒN. About these woods, far from the poplar-
    tree.

MER. What poplar mean ye ?

ŒN. Witness of the vows 'twixt him and me.
And come and wend a little way, and you shall
    see his skill.

MER. Sirs, tarry you.

ŒN.   Nay, let them go.

MER.   Nay, not unless you will.
Stay, nymph, and hark to what I say of him thou
    blamest so,
And, credit me, I've sad discourse to tell thee ere
    I go.
Know then, my pretty mops, that I hight Mercury,
The messenger of heaven, and hither fly,
To seize upon the man whom thou dost love,
To summon him before my father Jove,
To answer matter of great consequence :
And Jove himself will not be long from hence.

ŒN. Sweet Mercury, and have poor Œnon's cries
For Paris' fault y-pierced th' unpartial skies ?

MER. The same is he, that jolly shepherd's swain.

ŒN. His flock do graze upon Aurora's plain,
The colour of his coat is lusty green ;

That would these eyes of mine had never seen

His 'ticing curléd hair, his front of ivory,

Then had not I, poor I, bin unhappy.

 MER. No marvel, wench, although we cannot find
  him,

When all too late the Queen of Heaven doth mind
  him,

But if thou wilt have physic for thy sore,

Mind him who list, remember thou him no more.

And find some other game, and get thee gone ;

For here will lusty suitors come anon,

Too hot and lusty for thy dying vein,

Such as ne'er wont to make their suits in vain.

       [*Exit with the* CYCLOPS.

 Œn. I will go sit and pine under the poplar-tree,

And write my answer to his vow, that every eye may
  see.   [*Exit.*

SCENE II.

Enter VENUS, PARIS, *and a company of* SHEPHERDS.

 VEN. Shepherds, I am content, for this sweet
  shepherd's sake,

A strange revenge upon the maid and her disdain to
  take.

Let Colin's corpse be brought' in place, and buried
  in the plain,

And let this be the verse, " The love whom Thestylis
  hath slain."
And, trust me, I will chide my son for partiality,
That gave the swain so deep a wound, and let her
  scape him by.

> FIRST SHEP. Alas that ever Love was blind, to
> shoot so far amiss !
> VEN. Cupid my son was more to blame, the fault
> not mine, but his.   [*Exeunt* SHEPHERDS.
> PAR. O madam, if yourself would deign the
> handling of the bow,

Albeit it be a task, yourself more skill, more justice
  know.

> VEN. Sweet shepherd, didst thou ever love ?
> PAR.   Lady, a little once.
> VEN. And art thou changed ?
> PAR. Fair Queen of Love, I loved not all attonce.
> VEN. Well, wanton, wert thou wounded so deep
> as some have been,

It were a cunning cure to heal, and rueful to be
  seen.

> PAR. But tell me, gracious goddess, for a start and
> false offence

Hath Venus or her son the power at pleasure to
  dispense ?

> VEN. My boy, I will instruct thee in a piece of
> poetry,

That haply erst thou hast not heard : in hell there
    is a tree,
Where once a-day do sleep the souls of false for-
    sworen lovers,
With open hearts ; and thereabout in swarms the
    number hovers
Of poor forsaken ghosts, whose wings from off this
    tree do beat
Round drops of fiery Phlegethon to scorch false
    hearts with heat.
This pain did Venus and her son entreat the prince
    of hell
T' impose to such as faithless were to such as loved
    them well :
And, therefore, this, my lovely boy, fair Venus doth
    advise thee,
Be true and steadfast in thy love, beware thou do
    disguise thee,
For he that makes but love a jest, when pleaseth him
    to start
Shall feel those fiery water-drops consume his faith-
    less heart.
    PAR. Is Venus and her son so full of justice and
    severity ?
    VEN. Pity it were that love should not be linkéd
    with indifferency.
However lovers can exclaim for hard success in love,

Trust me, some more than common cause that
    painful hap doth move :
And Cupid's bow is not alone his triumph, but
    his rod ;
Nor is he only but a boy, he hight a mighty god ;
And they that do him reverence have reason for
    the same,
His shafts keep heaven and earth in awe, and
    shape rewards for shame.

PAR. And hath he reason to maintain why
    Colin died for love ?
VEN. Yea, reason good, I warrant thee, in right
    it might behove.
PAR. Then be the name of Love adored ; his bow
    is full of might,
His wounds are all but for desert, his laws are all
    but right.
VEN. Well, for this once me list apply my
    speeches to thy sense,
And Thestylis shall feel the pain for Love's sup-
    posed offence.

The SHEPHERDS *bring in* COLIN'S *hearse, singing.*

Welladay, welladay, poor Colin, thou art going to
    the ground,
    The love whom Thestylis hath slain,
    Hard heart, fair face, fraught with disdain,

Disdain in love a deadly wound.

    Wound her, sweet Love, so deep again,

    That she may feel the dying pain

    Of this unhappy shepherd's swain,

And die for love as Colin died, as Colin died.

VEN. Shepherds, abide; let Colin's corpse be witness of the pain

That Thestylis endures in love, a plague for her disdain.

Behold the organ of our wrath, this rusty churl is he ;

She dotes on his ill-favoured face, so much accursed is she.

Enter a foul crooked CHURL, *with* THESTYLIS *a fair* LASS, *who woos him, and sings an old song called "The Wooing of Colman:" he crabbedly refuses her, and goes out of place: she tarries behind.*

PAR. Ah, poor unhappy Thestylis, unpitied is thy pain !

VEN. Her fortune not unlike to hers whom cruel thou hast slain.

    [THESTYLIS *sings, and the* SHEPHERDS *reply.*

THE SONG.

THEST. The strange affects of my tormented
    heart,
Whom cruel love hath woful prisoner caught,
Whom cruel hate hath into bondage brought,
Whom wit no way of safe escape hath taught,
Enforce me say, in witness of my smart,
There is no pain to foul disdain in hardy suits of
    love.
    SHEP. There is no pain, &c.
    THEST. Cruel, farewell.
    SHEP. Cruel, farewell.
    THEST. Most cruel thou, of all that nature
    framed.
    SHEP. Most cruel, &c.
    THEST. To kill thy love with thy disdain.
    SHEP. To kill thy love with thy disdain.
    THEST. Cruel Disdain, so live thou named.
    SHEP. Cruel Disdain, &c.
    THEST. And let me die of Iphis' pain,
    SHEP. A life too good for thy disdain.
    THEST. Sith this my stars to me allot,
And thou thy love hast all forgot.
    SHEP. And thou, &c.   [*Exit* THESTYLIS.
        [*The grace of this song is in the* SHEP-
        HERDS' *echo to her verse.*

VEN. Now, shepherds, bury Colin's corpse, perfume his hearse with flowers,
And write what justice Venus did amid these woods
of yours.

[*The* SHEPHERDS *carry out* COLIN'S *hearse.*

How now, how cheers my lovely boy, after this
dump of love?

PAR. Such dumps, sweet lady, as bin these, are
deadly dumps to prove.

VEN. Cease, shepherd, there are other news, after
this melancholy:

My mind presumes some tempest toward upon the
speech of Mercury.

Enter MERCURY *with* VULCAN'S CYCLOPS.

MER. Fair Lady Venus, let me pardoned be,
That have of long bin well-beloved of thee,
If, as my office bids, myself first brings
To my sweet madam these unwelcome tidings.

VEN. What news, what tidings, gentle Mercury,
In midst of my delights, to trouble me?

MER. At Juno's suit, Pallas assisting her,
Sith both did join in suit to Jupiter,
Action is entered in the court of heaven;
And me, the swiftest of the planets seven,
With warrant they have thence despatched away,

To apprehend and find the man, they say,
That gave from them that self-same ball of gold,
Which, I presume, I do in place behold ;
Which man, unless my marks be taken wide,
Is he that sits so near thy gracious side.
This being so, it rests he go from hence,
Before the gods to answer his offence.

 VEN. What tale is this ? doth Juno and her mate
Pursue this shepherd with such deadly hate,
As what was then our general agreemént,
To stand unto they nill be now content ;
Let Juno jet, and Pallas play her part,
What here I have, I won it by desert ;
And heaven and earth shall both confounded be,
Ere wrong in this be done to him or me.

 MER. This little fruit, if Mercury can spell,
Will send, I fear, a world of souls to hell.

 VEN. What mean these Cyclops, Mercury ; is
  Vulcan waxed so fine,
To send his chimney-sweepers forth to fetter any
 friend of mine ?—
Abash not, shepherd, at the thing ; myself thy bail
 will be.—
He shall be present at the court of Jove, I warrant
 thee.

 MER. Venus, give me your pledge.

 VEN. My ceston, or my fan, or both ?

MER. [*taking her fan*]. Nay, this shall serve, your
    word to me as sure as is your oath,
At Diana's bower ; and, lady, if my wit or policy
May profit him, for Venus' sake let him make bold
    with Mercury.   [*Exit with the* CYCLOPS.
VEN. Sweet Paris, whereon dost thou muse ?
PAR. The angry heavens, for this fatal jar,
Name me the instrument of dire and deadly war.
                          [*Exeunt.*

ACT IV.

SCENE I.

Enter one of DIANA'S NYMPHS, *followed by* VULCAN.

VUL. Why, nymph, what need ye run so fast ?
    what though but black I be ?
I have more pretty knacks to please than every eye
    doth see ;   [smith,
And though I go not so upright, and though I am a
To make me gracious you may have some other thing
    therewith.

Enter BACCHUS.

BAC. Yea, Vulcan, will ye so indeed ?—Nay, turn,
    and tell him, child,   [beguiled,
He hath a mistress of his own who must not be

VUL. Why, sir, if Phœbe's dainty nymphs please
   Vulcan, in good sooth
Why may not Vulcan tread awry as well as Venus
   doth ?
   NYM. Ye shall not taint your troth for me : you
   wot it very well,   [hell.
All that be Dian's maids are vowed to halter apes in
   BAC. I'faith, i'faith, my gentle mops, but I do
   know a cast,
Lead apes who list, that we would help t' unhalter
   them as fast.
   NYM. Fie, fie, your skill is wondrous great !   Had
   thought the God of Wine
Had tended but his tubs and grapes, and not been
   half so fine.
   VUL. Gramercy for that quirk, my girl.
   BAC.   That's one of dainty's frumps.
   NYM. I pray, sir, take't with all amiss ; our cunning
   comes by lumps.
   VUL. Sh'ath capped his answer in the cue.
   NYM.   How says 'a, has she so ?
As well as she that capped your head to keep you
   warm below.
   VUL. Yea, then you will be curst I see.
   BAC.   Best let her even alone.
   NYM. Yea, gentle gods, and find some other
   string to harp upon.

BAC. Some other string! agreed, i'faith, some
    other pretty thing ;

'Twere shame fair maids should idle be : how say
    you, will ye sing ?

    NYM. Some rounds or merry roundelays, we sing
    no other songs ;

Your melancholic notes not to our country mirth
    belongs.

    VUL. Here comes a crew will help us trim.

    Enter MERCURY *with the* CYCLOPS.

MER. Yea, now our task is done.

BAC. Then, merry Mercury, more than time this
    round were well begun.

    [*They sing* "Hey down, down, down," &c.

    [*The song done, the* NYMPH *winds a horn
    in* VULCAN'S *ear, and runs out.*

VUL. A lightsome lass, I warrant her.

BAC.   A peevish elvish shroe.

MER. Have seen as far to come as near, for all
    her ranging so.

But, Bacchus, time well-spent I wot, our sacred
    father Jove,

With Phœbus and the God of War are met in
    Dian's grove.

VUL. Then we are here before them yet : but
   stay, the earth doth swell ;
God Neptune, too, (this hap is good,) doth meet the
   Prince of Hell.

PLUTO *ascends from below in his chair ;* NEPTUNE
   enters at another way.

PLU. What jars are these, that call the gods of
   heaven and hell below ?
NEP. It is a work of wit and toil to rule a lusty
   shroe.

Enter JUPITER, SATURN, APOLLO, MARS, JUNO,
   PALLAS, *and* DIANA.

JUP. Bring forth the man of Troy, that he may
   hear
Whereof he is to be arraignéd here.
NEP. Lo, where 'a comes, prepared to plead his
   case,
Under condúct of lovely Venus' grace !

Enter VENUS *with* PARIS.

MER. I have not seen a more alluring boy.
APOL. So beauty hight the wreck of Priam's Troy.
   [*The gods being set in* DIANA'S *bower ;*
      DIANA, JUNO, PALLAS, VENUS, *and*
      PARIS *stand on sides before them.*

VEN. Lo, sacred Jove, at Juno's proud complaint,
As erst I gave my pledge to Mercury,
I bring the man whom he did late attaint,
To answer his indictment orderly ;
And crave this grace of this immortal senate,
That ye allow the man his advocate.

    PAL. That may not be ; the laws of heaven
      deny
A man to plead or answer by attorney.

    VEN. Pallas, thy doom is all too peremptory.

    APOL. Venus, that favour is denied him flatly :
He is a man, and therefore by our laws,
Himself, without his aid, must plead his cause.

    VEN. Then 'bash not, shepherd, in so good a
      case ;
And friends thou hast, as well as foes, in place.

    JUNO. Why, Mercury, why do ye not indict
      him ?

    VEN. Soft, gentle Juno, I pray you, do not bite
      him.

    JUNO. Nay, gods, I trow, you are like to have
      great silence,
Unless this parrot be commanded hence.

    JUP. Venus, forbear, be still.—Speak, Mercury.

    VEN. If Juno jangle, Venus will reply.

    MER. Paris, King Priam's son, thou art arraigned
      of partiality,

Of sentence partial and unjust; for that without
    indifferency,
Beyond desert or merit fair, as thine accusers say,
From them, to Lady Venus here, thou gav'st the
    prize away :
What is thine answer ?

PARIS' ORATION TO THE COUNCIL OF THE GODS.

Sacred and just, thou great and dreadful Jove,
And you thrice-reverend powers, whom love nor
    hate
May wrest awry ; if this to me a man,
This fortune fatal be, that I must plead
For safe excusal of my guiltless thought,
The honour more makes my mishap the less,
That I a man must plead before the gods—
Gracious forbearers of the world's amiss—
For her, whose beauty how it hath enticed,
This heavenly senate may with me aver.
But sith nor that nor this may do me boot,
And for myself myself must speaker be,
A mortal man amidst this heavenly presence ;
Let me not shape a long defence to them
That ben beholders of my guiltless thoughts.
Then for the deed, that I may not deny,
Wherein consists the full of mine offence,

I did upon command ; if then I erred,
I did no more than to a man belonged.
And if, in verdict of their forms divine,
My dazzled eye did swerve or surfeit more
On Venus' face than any face of theirs,
It was no partial fault, but fault of his,
Belike, whose eyesight not so perfect was
As might discern the brightness of the rest.
And if it were permitted unto men,
Ye gods, to parley with your secret thoughts,
There ben that sit upon that sacred seat,
That would with Paris err in Venus' praise.
But let me cease to speak of error here ;
Sith what my hand, the organ of my heart,
Did give with good agreement of mine eye,
My tongue is void with process to maintain.

PLU. A jolly shepherd, wise and eloquent.

PAR. First, then, arraigned of partiality,
Paris replies, " Unguilty of the fact " ;
His reason is, because he knew no more
Fair Venus' ceston than Dame Juno's mace,
Nor never saw wise Pallas' crystal shield.
Then, as I looked, I loved and liked attonce,
And as it was referred from them to me,
To give the prize to her whose beauty best
My fancy did commend, so did I praise
And judge as might my dazzled eye discern.

NEP. A piece of art, that cunningly, perdy,
Refers the blame to weakness of his eye.

PAR. Now, for I must add reason for my deed,
Why Venus rather pleased me of the three ;
First, in the entrails of my mortal ears,
The question standing upon Beauty's blaze,
The name of her that hight the Queen of Love,
Methought in beauty should not be excelled.
Had it been destinéd to Majesty,
(Yet will I not rob Venus of her grace,)
Then stately Juno might have borne the ball.
Had it to Wisdom been intituléd,
My human wit had given it Pallas then.
But sith unto the fairest of the three
That power, that threw it for my farther ill,
Did dedicate this ball ; and safest durst
My shepherd's skill adventure, as I thought,
To judge of form and beauty rather than
Of Juno's state or Pallas' worthiness,
That learned to ken the fairest of the flock,
And praiséd beauty but by nature's aim ;
Behold, to Venus Paris gave this fruit,
A daysman chosen there by full consent,
And heavenly powers should not repent their
          deeds.
Where it is said, beyond desert of hers
I honoured Venus with this golden prize,

Ye gods, alas, what can a mortal man
Discern betwixt the sacred gifts of heaven ?
Or, if I may with reverence reason thus :
Suppose I gave, and judged corruptly then,
For hope of that that best did please my thought,
This apple not for beauty's praise alone ;
I might offend, sith I was pardonéd,
And tempted more than ever creature was
With wealth, with beauty, and with chivalry,
And so preferred beauty before them all,
The thing that hath enchanted heaven itself.
And for the one, contentment is my wealth ;
A shell of salt will serve a shepherd swain,
A slender banquet in a homely scrip,
And water running from the silver spring.
For arms, they dread no foes that sit so low ;
A thorn can keep the wind from off my back,
A sheep-cote thatched a shepherd's palace hight.
Of tragic Muses shepherds con no skill ;
Enough is them, if Cupid be displeased,
To sing his praise on slender oaten pipe.
And thus, thrice-reverend, have I told my tale,
And crave the torment of my guiltless soul
To be measúréd by my faultless thought.
If warlike Pallas or the Queen of Heaven
Sue to reverse my sentence by appeal,
Be it as please your majesties divine ;

The wrong, the hurt, not mine, if any be,
But hers whose beauty claimed the prize of me.

[PARIS *having ended*, JUPITER *speaks.*

JUP. Venus, withdraw your shepherd for a space,
Till he again be called for into place.

[*Exeunt* VENUS *and* PARIS.

Juno, what will ye after this reply,
But doom with sentence of indifferency?
And if you will but justice in the cause,
The man must quitted be by heaven's laws.

JUNO. Yea, gentle Jove, when Juno's suits are
    moved,
Then heaven may see how well she is beloved.

APOL. But, madam, fits it majesty divine
In any sort from justice to decline?

PAL. Whether the man be guilty, yea or no,
That doth not hinder our appeal, I trow.

JUNO. Phœbus, I wot, amid this heavenly crew,
There be that have to say as well as you.

APOL. And, Juno, I with them, and they with me,
In law and right must needfully agree.

PAL. I grant ye may agree, but be content
To doubt on regard of your agreemént.

PLU. And if ye marked, the man in his defence
Said thereof as 'a might with reverence.

VUL. And did that very well, I promise ye.

JUNO. No doubt, sir, you could note it cunningly.

SAT. Well, Juno, if ye will appeal, ye may,
But first despatch the shepherd hence away.

MARS. Then Vulcan's dame is like to have the
wrong.

JUNO. And that in passion doth to Mars belong,

JUP. Call Venus and the shepherd in again.

BAC. And rid the man that he may know his
pain.

APOL. His pain, his pain, his never-dying pain,
A cause to make a many more complain.

MERCURY *brings in* VENUS *and* PARIS.

JUP. Shepherd, thou hast been heard with equity
and law,
And for thy stars do thee to other calling draw,
We here dismiss thee hence, by order of our senate:
Go take thy way to Troy, and there abide thy fate.

VEN. Sweet shepherd, with such luck in love, while
thou dost live,
As may the Queen of Love to any lover give.

PAR. My luck is loss, howe'er my love do speed:
I fear me Paris shall but rue his deed.   [*Exit.*

APOL. From Ida woods now wends the shepherd's
boy,
That in his bosom carries fire to Troy.

JUP. Venus, these ladies do appeal, you see,
And that they may appeal the gods agree:

C

It resteth, then, that you be well content
To stand in this to our final judgment ;
And if King Priam's son did well in this,
The law of heaven will not lead amiss.

   VEN. But, sacred Jupiter, might thy daughter
      choose,
She might with reason this appeal refuse :
Yet, if they be unmovéd in their shames,
Be it a stain and blemish to their names :
A deed, too, far unworthy of the place,
Unworthy Pallas' lance or Juno's mace :
And if to beauty it bequeathéd be,
I doubt not but it will return to me.
                             [Lays down the ball.

   PAL. Venus, there is no more ado than so,
It resteth where the gods do it bestow.

   NEP. But, ladies, under favour of your rage,
Howe'er it be, you play upon the vantage.

   JUP. Then, dames, that we more freely may
      debate,
And hear th' indifferent sentence of this senate,
Withdraw you from this presence for a space,
Till we have throughly questioned of the case :
Dian shall be your guide ; nor shall you need
Yourselves t' inquire how things do here succeed ;
We will, as we resolve, give you to know,
By general doom how everything doth go.

DIA. Thy will, my wish.—Fair ladies, will ye
wend ?

JUNO. Beshrew her whom this sentence doth
offend.

VEN. Now, Jove, be just ; and, gods, you that be
Venus' friends,

If you have ever done her wrong, then may you
make amends.

[*Exeunt* DIANA, JUNO, PALLAS, *and* VENUS.

JUP. Venus is fair, Pallas and Juno too.

VUL. But tell me now without some more ado,
Who is the fairest she, and do not flatter.

PLU. Upon comparison hangs all the matter :
That done, the quarrel and the strife were ended.

MARS. Because 'tis known, the quarrel is pre-
tended.

VUL. Mars, you have reason for your speech,
perdy ;
My dame, I trow, is fairest in your eye.

MARS. Or, Vulcan, I should do her double wrong.

SAT. About a toy we tarry here too long.
Give it by voices, voices give the odds ;
A trifle so to trouble all the gods !

NEP. Believe me, Saturn, be it so for me,

BAC. For me.

PLU. For me.

MARS. For me, if Jove agree

MER. And, gentle gods, I am indifferent ;
But then I know who's likely to be shent.

APOL. Thrice-reverend gods, and thou, immortal
Jove,
If Phœbus may, as him doth much behove,
Be licenséd, according to our laws,
To speak uprightly in this doubted cause,
(Sith women's wits work men's unceasing woes,)
To make them friends, that now bin friendless
foes,
And peace to keep with them, with us, and all,
That make their title to this golden ball ;
(Nor think, ye gods, my speech doth derogate
From sacred power of this immortal senate ;)
Refer this sentence where it doth belong :
In this, say I, fair Phœbe hath the wrong ;
Not that I mean her beauty bears the prize,
But that the holy law of heaven denies
One god to meddle in another's power ;
And this befell so near Diana's bower,
As for th' appeasing this unpleasant grudge,
In my conceit, she hight the fittest judge.
If Jove control not Pluto's hell with charms,
If Mars have sovereign power to manage arms,
If Bacchus bear no rule in Neptune's sea,
Nor Vulcan's fire doth Saturn's scythe obey,
Suppress not then, 'gainst law and equity,

Diana's power in her own territory,
Whose regiment, amid her sacred bowers,
As proper hight as any rule of yours.
Well may we so wipe all the speech away,
That Pallas, Juno, Venus, hath to say,
And answer that, by justice of our laws
We were not suffered to conclude the cause.
And this to me most equal doom appears,
A woman to be judge among her feres.

MER. Apollo hath found out the only mean
To rid the blame from us and trouble clean.

VUL. We are beholding to his sacred wit.

JUP. I can commend and well allow of it ;
And so derive the matter from us all,
That Dian have the giving of the ball.

VUL. So Jove may clearly excuse him in the
case,
Where Juno else would chide and brawl apace.
[*They all rise.*

MER. And now it were some cunning to divine
To whom Diana will this prize resign.

VUL. Sufficeth me, it shall be none of mine.

BAC. Vulcan, though thou be black, thou'rt nothing
fine.

VUL. Go bathe thee, Bacchus, in a tub of wine ;
The ball's as likely to be mine as thine.   [*Exeunt.*

ACT V.

SCENE I.

Enter DIANA, JUNO, PALLAS, *and* VENUS.

DIA. Lo, ladies, far beyond my hope and will,
    you see,
This thankless office is imposed to me ;
Wherein if you will rest as well content,
As Dian will be judge indifferent,
My equal doom shall none of you offend,
And of this quarrel make a final end :
And therefore, whether you be lief or loth,
Confirm your promise with some sacred oath.
    PAL. Phœbe, chief mistress of this sylvan chase,
Whom gods have chosen to conclude the case
That yet in balance undecided lies,
Touching bestowing of this golden prize,
I give my promise and mine oath withal,
By Styx, by heaven's power imperial,
By all that 'longs to Pallas' deity,
Her shield, her lance, ensigns of chivalry,
Her sacred wreath of olive and of bay,
Her crested helm, and else what Pallas may,
That whereso'er this ball of purest gold,

That chaste Diana here in hand doth hold,
Unpartially her wisdom shall bestow,
Without mislike or quarrel any mo,
Pallas shall rest content and satisfied,
And say the best desert doth there abide.

JUNO. And here I promise and protest withal,
By Styx, by heaven's power imperial,
By all that 'longs to Juno's deity,
Her crown, her mace, ensigns of majesty,
Her spotless marriage-rites, her league divine,
And by that holy name of Proserpine,
That wheresoe'er this ball of purest gold,
That chaste Diana here in hand doth hold,
Unpartially her wisdom shall bestow,
Without mislike or quarrel any mo,
Juno shall rest content and satisfied,
And say the best desert doth there abide.

VEN. And, lovely Phœbe, for I know thy doom
Will be no other than shall thee become,
Behold, I take thy dainty hand to kiss,
And with my solemn oath confirm my promise,
By Styx, by Jove's immortal empery,
By Cupid's bow, by Venus' myrtle-tree,
By Vulcan's gift, my ceston and my fan,
By this red rose, whose colour first began
When erst my wanton boy (the more his blame)
Did draw his bow awry and hurt his dame,

By all the honour and the sacrifice
That from Cithæron and from Paphos rise,
That wheresoe'er this ball of purest gold,
That chaste Diana here in hand doth hold,
Unpartially her wisdom shall bestow,
Without mislike or quarrel any mo,
Venus shall rest content and satisfied,
And say the best desert doth there abide.

> [DIANA, *having taken their oaths, speaks.*
> DIANA *describes the Nymph* ELIZA, *a*
> *figure of the* QUEEN.

DIA. It is enough, and, goddesses, attend.
There wons within these pleasant shady woods,
Where neither storm nor sun's distemperature
Have power to hurt by cruel heat or cold,
Under the climate of the milder heaven ;
Where seldom lights Jove's angry thunderbolt,
For favour of that sovereign earthly peer ;
Where whistling winds make music 'mong the trees,
Far from disturbance of our country gods,
Amids the cypress-springs, a gracious nymph,
That honours Dian for her chastity,
And likes the labours well of Phœbe's groves.
The place Elysium hight, and of the place
Her name that governs there Eliza is ;
A kingdom that may well compare with mine,
An ancient seat of kings, a second Troy,

Y-compassed round with a commodious sea :
Her people are y-clepéd Angeli,
Or, if I miss, a letter is the most.
She giveth laws of justice and of peace ;
And on her head, as fits her fortune best,
She wears a wreath of laurel, gold and palm ;
Her robes of purple and of scarlet dye ;
Her veil of white, as best befits a maid :
Her ancestors live in the House of Fame :
She giveth arms of happy victory,
And flowers to deck her lions crowned with gold.
This peerless nymph, whom heaven and earth
        belove,
This paragon, this only, this is she,
In whom do meet so many gifts in one,
On whom our country gods so often gaze,
In honour of whose name the Muses sing :
In·state Queen Juno's peer, for power in arms
And virtues of the mind Minerva's mate,
As fair and lovely as the Queen of Love,
As chaste as Dian in her chaste desires :
The same is she, if Phœbe do no wrong,
To whom this ball in merit doth belong.

    PAL. If this be she whom some Zabeta call,
To whom thy wisdom well bequeaths the ball,
I can remember, at her day of birth,
How Flora with her flowers strewed the earth,

How every power with heavenly majesty
In person honoured that solemnity.

JUNO. The lovely Graces were not far away,
They threw their balm for triumph of the day.

VEN. The Fates, against their kind, began a cheer-
ful song,
And vowed her life with favour to prolong.
Then first gan Cupid's eyesight wexen dim ;
Belike Eliza's beauty blinded him.
To this fair nymph, not earthly, but divine,
Contents it me my honour to resign.

PAL. To this fair queen, so beautiful and wise,
Pallas bequeaths her title in the prize.

JUNO. To her whom Juno's looks so well become,
The Queen of Heaven yields at Phœbe's doom ;
And glad I am Diana found the art,
Without offence so well to please desert.

DIA. Then mark my tale. The usual time is nigh,
When wont the Dames of Life and Destiny,
In robes of cheerful colours, to repair
To this renownéd queen so wise and fair,
With pleasant songs this peerless nymph to greet :
Clotho lays down her distaff at her feet,
And Lachesis doth pull the thread at length,
The third with favour gives it stuff and strength,
And for contráry kind affords her leave,
As her best likes, her web of life to weave.

This time we will attend, and in mean while
With some sweet song the tediousness beguile.

The Music sounds, and the NYMPHS *within sing or*
solfa with voices and instruments awhile. Then
enter CLOTHO, LACHESIS, *and* ATROPOS, *sing-*
ing as follows: the state being in place.

THE SONG.

CLO. Humanæ vitæ filum sic volvere Parcæ.

LACH. Humanæ vitæ filum sic tendere Parcæ.

ATRO. Humanæ vitæ filum sic scindere Parcæ.

CLO. Clotho colum bajulat.

LACH.   Lachesis trahit.

ATRO.   Atropos occat.

TRES SIMUL. Vive diu felix votis hominumque
deumque,

Corpore, mente, libro, doctissima, candida, casta.

       [*They lay down their properties at the*
         QUEEN'S *feet.*

CLO. Clotho colum pedibus.

LACH. Lachesis tibi pendula fila.   [offert.

ATRO. Et fatale tuis manibus ferrum Atropos

TRES SIMUL. Vive diu felix, &c.

       [*The song being ended,* CLOTHO *speaks to*
        the QUEEN.

CLO. Gracious and wise, fair Queen of rare
　　renown,
Whom heaven and earth belove, amid thy train,
Noble and lovely peers, to honour thee
And do thee favour more than may belong
By nature's law to any earthly wight,
Behold continuance of our yearly due :
Th' unpartial Dames of Destiny, we meet,
As have the gods and we agreed in one,
In reverence of Eliza's noble name ;
And humbly, lo, her distaff Clotho yields !

LACH. Her spindle Lachesis, and her fatal reel,
Lays down in reverence at Eliza's feet.
Te tamen in terris unam tria numina Divam
Invita statuunt naturæ lege sorores,
Et tibi non aliis didicerunt parcere Parcæ.

ATRO. Dame Atropos, according as her feres,
To thee, fair Queen, resigns her fatal knife :
Live long the noble phœnix of our age,
Our fair Eliza, our Zabeta fair !

DIA. And, lo, beside this rare solemnity,
And sacrifice these dames are wont to do,
A favour, far indeed contráry kind,
Bequeathéd is unto thy worthiness,—
This prize from heaven and heavenly goddesses !

　　　　　[*Delivers the ball of gold to the* QUEEN'S
　　　　　　own hands.

Accept it, then, thy due by Dian's doom,
Praise of the Wisdom, Beauty, and the State,
That best becomes thy peerless excellency.

VEN. So, fair Eliza, Venus doth resign
The honour of this honour to be thine.

JUNO. So is the Queen of Heaven content likewise
To yield to thee her title in the prize.

PAL. So Pallas yields the praise hereof to thee,
For Wisdom, princely State, and peerless Beauty.

EPILOGUS.

OMNES SIMUL. Vive diu felix, votis hominumque
    deumque,
Corpore, mente, libro, doctissima, candida, casta.

                        [Exeunt Omnes.

THE LOVE OF

DAVID AND FAIR BETHSABE,

WITH THE TRAGEDY OF ABSALON.

A.D. 1599 (Dyce) — See supra p. 3.

DRAMATIS PERSONÆ.

DAVID.

AMNON, *son of* DAVID *by* AHINOAM.

CHILEAB, *son of* DAVID *by* ABIGAIL.

ABSALON, *son of* DAVID *by* MAACAH.

ADONIA, *son of* DAVID *by* HAGITH.

SALOMON, *son of* DAVID *by* BETHSABE.

JOAB, *captain of the host to* DAVID, ABISAI, } *nephews of* DAVID *and sons of his sister* ZERUIAH.

AMASA, *nephew of* DAVID *and son of his sister* ABIGAIL; *captain of the host to* ABSALON.

JONADAB, *nephew of* DAVID *and son of his brother* SHIMEAH; *friend to* AMNON.

URIAS, *husband of* BETHSABE, *and a warrior in* DAVID'S *army.*

NATHAN, *a prophet.*

SADOC, *high-priest.*

AHIMAAS, *his son.*

ABIATHAR, *a priest.*

JONATHAN, *his son.*

ACHITOPHEL, *chief counsellor to* ABSALON.

CUSAY.

ITHAY.

SEMEI.

JETHRAY.

HANON, *King of Ammon.*

MACHAAS, *King of Gath.*

Messenger, Soldiers, Shepherds, and Attendants.

THAMAR, *daughter of* DAVID *by* MAACAH.

BETHSABE, *wife of* URIAS.

WOMAN OF THECOA.

CONCUBINES TO DAVID.

MAID TO BETHSABE.

CHORUS.

ACT I.

PROLOGUS.

OF Israel's sweetest singer now I sing,
His holy style and happy victories ;
Whose Muse was dipt in that inspiring dew
Archangels stilléd from the breath of Jove,
Decking her temples with the glorious flowers
Heavens rained on tops of Sion and Mount Sinai.
Upon the bosom of his ivory lute
The cherubins and angels laid their breasts ;
And, when his consecrated fingers struck
The golden wires of his ravishing harp,
He gave alarum to the host of heaven,
That, winged with lightning, brake the clouds, and
    cast
Their crystal armour at his conquering feet.
Of this sweet poet, Jove's musician,
And of his beauteous son, I press to sing.
Then help, divine Adonai, to conduct
Upon the wings of my well-tempered verse
The hearers' minds above the towers of heaven,
And guide them so in this thrice-haughty flight,
Their mounting feathers scorch not with the fire

That none can temper but thy holy hand :
To thee for succour flies my feeble Muse,
And at thy feet her iron pen doth use.

SCENE I.—*Without* KING DAVID'S *Palace at Jerusalem.*

*The Prologue-speaker, before going out, draws a cur-
tain and discovers* BETHSABE, *with her* MAID,
bathing over a spring : she sings, and DAVID
sits above viewing her.

THE SONG.

Hot sun, cool fire, tempered with sweet air,
Black shade, fair nurse, shadow my white hair :
Shine, sun ; burn, fire ; breathe, air, and ease me ;
Black shade, fair nurse, shroud me, and please me :
Shadow, my sweet nurse, keep me from burning,
Make not my glad cause cause of my mourning.
> Let not my·beauty's fire
> Inflame unstaid desire,
> Nor pierce any bright eye
> That wandereth lightly.

BETH. Come, gentle Zephyr, tricked with those
perfumes
That erst in Eden sweetened Adam's love,

And stroke my bosom with thy silken fan :
This shade, sun-proof, is yet no proof for thee ;
Thy body, smoother than this waveless spring,
And purer than the substance of the same,
Can creep through that his lances cannot pierce :
Thou, and thy sister, soft and sacred Air,
Goddess of life and governess of health,
Keep every fountain fresh and arbour sweet ;
No brazen gate her passage can repulse,
Nor bushy thicket bar thy subtle breath :
Then deck thee with thy loose delightsome robes,
And on thy wings bring delicate perfumes,
To play the wanton with us through the leaves.

   DAV. What tunes, what words, what looks, what
     wonders pierce,
My soul, incenséd with a sudden fire ?
What tree, what shade, what spring, what paradise,
Enjoys the beauty of so fair a dame ?
Fair Eva, placed in perfect happiness,
Lending her praise-notes to the liberal heavens,
Struck with the accents of archangels' tunes,
Wrought not more pleasure to her husband's
     thoughts
Than this fair woman's words and notes to mine.
May that sweet plain that bears her pleasant
     weight
Be still enamelled with discoloured flowers ;

That precious fount bear sand of purest gold ;
And, for the pebble, let the silver streams
That pierce earth's bowels to maintain the source,
Play upon rubies, sapphires, chrysolites ;
The brims let be embraced with golden curls
Of moss that sleeps with sound the waters make
For joy to feed the fount with their recourse ;
Let all the grass that beautifies her bower
Bear manna every morn instead of dew,
Or let the dew be sweeter far than that
That hangs, like chains of pearl, on Hermon hill,
Or balm which trickled from old Aaron's beard.—
Cusay, come up, and serve thy lord the king.

Enter CUSAY *above.*

Cu. What service doth my lord the king
    command ?

DAV. See, Cusay, see the flower of Israel,
The fairest daughter that obeys the king
In all the land the Lord subdued to me ;
Fairer than Isaac's lover at the well,
Brighter than inside-bark of new-hewn cedar,
Sweeter than flames of fine-perfuméd myrrh,
And comelier than the silver clouds that dance
On Zephyr's wings before the King of Heaven.

Cu. Is it not Bethsabe the Hethite's wife,
Urias, now at Rabbah siege with Joab ?

DAV. Go know, and bring her quickly to the
king ;

Tell her, her graces have found grace with him.

CU. I will, my lord.   [*Exit.*

DAV. Bright Bethsabe shall wash, in David's
bower,

In water mixed with purest almond-flower,

And bathe her beauty in the milk of kids :

Bright Bethsabe gives earth to my desires ;

Verdure to earth ; and to that verdure flowers ;

To flowers sweet odours ; and to odours wings

That carry pleasures to the hearts of kings.

Enter CUSAY, *below, to* BETHSABE, *she starting as
something affright.*

CU. Fair Bethsabe, the King of Israel

From forth his princely tower hath seen thee
bathe ;

And thy sweet graces have found grace with him :

Come, then, and kneel unto him where he stands ;

The king is gracious, and hath liberal hands.

BETH. Ah, what is Bethsabe to please the king ?

Or what is David, that he should desire,

For fickle beauty's sake, his servant's wife ?

CU. David, thou knowest, fair dame, is wise and
just,

Elected to the heart of Israel's God ;
Then do not thou expostulate with him
For any action that contents his soul.

BETH. My lord the king, elect to God's own
  heart,
Should not his gracious jealousy incense
Whose thoughts are chaste : I hate incontinence.

CU. Woman, thou wrong'st the king, and
  doubt'st his honour,
Whose truth maintains the crown of Israel,
Making him stay that bade me bring thee straight.

BETH. The king's poor handmaid will obey my
  lord.

CU. Then come, and do thy duty to his grace ;
And do what seemeth favour in his sight.

      [*Exit, below, with* BETHSABE.

DAV. Now comes my lover tripping like the roe,
And brings my longings tangled in her hair.
To joy her love I'll build a kingly bower,
Seated in hearing of a hundred streams,
That, for their homage to her sovereign joys,
Shall, as the serpents fold into their nests
In oblique turnings, wind their nimble waves
About the circles of her curious walks ;
And with their murmur summon easeful sleep
To lay his golden sceptre on her brows.—
Open the doors, and entertain my love ;

Open, I say, and, as you open, sing,
Welcome, fair Bethsabe, King David's darling.

Enter, above, CUSAY *with* BETHSABE.

Welcome, fair Bethsabe, King David's darling.
Thy bones' fair covering, erst discovered fair,
And all mine eyes with all thy beauties pierced :
As heaven's bright eye burns most when most he
        climbs
The crookéd zodiac with his fiery sphere,
And shineth furthest from this earthly globe ;
So, since thy beauty scorched my conquered soul,
I called thee nearer for my nearer cure.

    BETH. Too near, my lord, was your unarméd
        heart
When furthest off my hapless beauty pierced ;
And would this dreary day had turned to night,
Or that some pitchy cloud had cloaked the sun,
Before their lights had caused my lord to see
His name disparaged and my chastity !

    DAV. My love, if want of love have left thy
        soul
A sharper sense of honour than thy king,
(For love leads princes sometimes from their seats,)
As erst my heart was hurt, displeasing thee,
So come and taste thy ease with easing me.

BETH. One medicine cannot heal our different
    harms ;
But rather make both rankle at the bone :
Then let the king be cunning in his cure,
Lest flattering both, both perish in his hand.

    DAV. Leave it to me, my dearest Bethsabe,
Whose skill is conversant in deeper cures.—
And, Cusay, haste thou to my servant Joab,
Commanding him to send Urias home
With all the speed can possibly be used.

    CU. Cusay will fly about the king's desire.

                      [*Exeunt.*

SCENE II.—*Before the Walls of Rabbah, with a tower
    of the Palace of Hanon, King of Ammon.*

Enter JOAB, ABISAI, URIAS, *and others, with drum
    and ensign.*

    JOAB. Courage, ye mighty men of Israel,
And charge your fatal instruments of war
Upon the bosoms of proud Ammon's sons,
That have disguised your king's ambassadors,
Cut half their beards and half their garments off,
In spite of Israel and his daughters' sons !
Ye fight the holy battles of Jehovah,
King David's God, and ours, and Jacob's God

That guides your weapons to their conquering
    strokes,
Orders your footsteps, and directs your thoughts
To stratagems that harbour victory :
He casts His sacred eyesight from on high,
And sees your foes run seeking for their deaths,
Laughing their labours and their hopes to scorn ;
While 'twixt your bodies and their blunted swords
He puts on armour of His honour's proof,
And makes their weapons wound the senseless
    winds.

    ABIS. Before this city Rabbah we will lie,
And shoot forth shafts as thick and dangerous
As was the hail that Moses mixed with fire,
And threw with fury round about the fields,
Devouring Pharaoh's friends and Egypt's fruits.

    UR. First, mighty captains, Joab and Abisai,
Let us assault, and scale this kingly tower,
Where all their conduits and their fountains
    are ;
Then we may easily take the city too.

    JOAB. Well hath Urias counselled our attempts ;
And as he spake us, so assault the tower :
Let Hanon now, the king of Ammon's sons,
Repulse our conquering passage if he dare.

Enter HANON, MACHAAS, *and others, upon the walls.*

HA. What would the shepherd's-dogs of Israel
Snatch from the mighty issue of King Ammon,
The valiant Ammonites and haughty Syrians ?
'Tis not your late successive victories
Can make us yield, or quail our courages ;
But if ye dare assay to scale this tower,
Our angry swords shall smite ye to the ground,
And venge our losses on your hateful lives.

JOAB. Hanon, thy father Nahas gave relief
To holy David in his hapless exile,
Livéd his fixéd date, and died in peace :
But thou, instead of reaping his reward,
Hast trod it under foot, and scorned our king ;
Therefore thy days shall end with violence,
And to our swords thy vital blood shall cleave.

MACH. Hence, thou that bear'st poor Israel's
    shepherd's-hook,
The proud lieutenant of that base-born king,
And keep within the compass of his fold ;
For, if ye seek to feed on Ammon's fruits,
And stray into the Syrians' fruitful meads,
The mastiffs of our land shall worry ye,
And pull the weasands from your greedy throats.

ABIS. Who can endure these pagans' blasphemies ?

UR. My soul repines at this disparagement.

JOAB. Assault, ye valiant men of David's host,

And beat these railing dastards from their doors.

      [*Assault, and they win the tower ; and then*

         JOAB *speaks above.*

Thus have we won the tower, which we will keep,

Maugre the sons of Ammon and of Syria.

Enter CUSAY *below.*

CU. Where is Lord Joab, leader of the host ?

JOAB. Here is Lord Joab, leader of the host.

Cusay, come up, for we have won the hold.

  CU. In happy hour, then, is Cusay come.

               [CUSAY *goes up.*

JOAB. What news, then, brings Lord Cusay from

    the king ?

  CU. His majesty commands thee out of hand

To send him home Urias from the wars,

For matter of some service he should do.

  UR. 'Tis for no choler hath surprised the king,

I hope, Lord Cusay, 'gainst his servant's truth ?

  CU. No; rather to prefer Urias' truth.

  JOAB. Here, take him with thee, then, and go in

    peace ;

And tell my lord the king that I have fought

Against the city Rabbah with success,

And scaléd where the royal palace is,
The conduit-heads and all their sweetest springs;
Then let him come in person to these walls,
With all the soldiers he can bring besides,
And take the city as his own exploit,
Lest I surprise it, and the people give
The glory of the conquest to my name.

CU. We will, Lord Joab; and great Israel's God
Bless in thy hands the battles of our king!

JOAB. Farewell, Urias; haste away the king.

UR. As sure as Joab breathes a victor here,
Urias will haste him and his own return.

     [*Exeunt* CUSAY *and* URIAS.

ABIS. Let us descend, and ope the palace gate,
Taking our soldiers in to keep the hold.

JOAB. Let us, Abisai:—and, ye sons of Judah,
Be valiant, and maintain your victory.   [*Exeunt.*

SCENE III.—*Within the Palace of* KING DAVID.

Enter AMNON, JONADAB, JETHRAY, *and* AMNON'S
     PAGE.

JONAD. What means my lord, the king's belovéd
  son,
That wears upon his right triumphant arm
The power of Israel for a royal favour,

That holds upon the tables of his hands
Banquets of honour and all thought's content,
To suffer pale and grisly abstinence
To sit and feed upon his fainting cheeks,
And suck away the blood that cheers his looks ?

AM. Ah, Jonadab, it is my sister's looks,
On whose sweet beauty I bestow my blood,
That make me look so amorously lean ;
Her beauty having seized upon my heart,
So merely consecrate to her content,
Sets now such guard about his vital blood,
And views the passage with such piercing eyes,
That none can scape to cheer my pining cheeks,
But all is thought too little for her love.

JONAD. Then from her heart thy looks shall be
    relieved,
And thou shalt joy her as thy soul desires.

AM. How can it be, my sweet friend Jonadab,
Since Thamar is a virgin and my sister ?

JONAD. Thus it shall be : lie down upon thy bed,
Feigning thee fever-sick and ill-at-ease ;
And when the king shall come to visit thee,
Desire thy sister Thamar may be sent
To dress some dainties for thy malady :
Then when thou hast her solely with thyself,
Enforce some favour to thy manly love.
See where she comes : entreat her in with thee.

Enter THAMAR.

THA. What aileth Amnon, with such sickly looks
To daunt the favour of his lovely face ?
　AM. Sweet Thamar, sick, and wish some whole-
　　some cates
Dressed with the cunning of thy dainty hands.
　THA. That hath the king commanded at my
　　hands :
Then come and rest thee, while I make thee ready
Some dainties easeful to thy crazéd soul.
　AM. I go, sweet sister, eknéd with thy sight.
　　　[*Exeunt* THAMAR, AMNON, JETHRAY, *and*
　　　PAGE.
　JONAD. Why should a prince, whose power may
　　command,
Obey the rebel passions of his love,
When they contend but 'gainst his conscience,
And may be governed or suppressed by will ?
Now, Amnon, loose those loving knots of blood,
That sucked the courage from thy kingly heart,
And give it passage to thy withered cheeks.
Now, Thamar, ripened are the holy fruits .
That grew on plants of thy virginity ;
And rotten is thy name in Israel :
Poor Thamar, little did thy lovely hands

Foretell an action of such violence
As to contend with Amnon's lusty arms
Sinewed with vigour of his kindless love :
Fair Thamar, now dishonour hunts thy foot,
And follows thee through every covert shade,
Discovering thy shame and nakedness,
Even from the valleys of Jehosaphat
Up to the lofty mounts of Lebanon ;
Where cedars, stirred with anger of the winds,
Sounding in storms the tale of thy disgrace,
Tremble with fury, and with murmur shake   `
Earth with their feet and with their heads the
        heavens,
Beating the clouds into their swiftest rack
To bear this wonder round about the world.   [*Exit.*

Re-enter AMNON *thrusting out* THAMAR, *and*
· JETHRAY.

    AM. Hence from my bed, whose sight offends
        my soul
As doth the parbreak of disgorgéd bears !
    THA. Unkind, unprincely, and unmanly Amnon,
To force, and then refuse thy sister's love,
Adding unto the fright of thy offence
The baneful torment of my published shame !
O, do not this dishonour to thy love,

Nor clog thy soul with such increasing sin !
This second evil far exceeds the first.

   AM. Jethray, come thrust this woman from my
     sight,
And bolt the door upon her if she strive.   [*Exit.*

   JETH. Go, madam, go ; away ; you must be gone ;
My lord hath done with you : I pray, depart.
                   [*Shuts her out.—Exit.*

   THA. Whither, alas, ah, whither shall I fly,
With folded arms and all-amazéd soul ?
Cast as was Eva from that glorious soil,
(Where all delights sat bating, winged with thoughts,
Ready to nestle in her naked breasts,)
To bare and barren vales with floods made waste,
To desert woods, and hills with lightning scorched,
With death, with shame, with hell, with horror
     sit ;
There will I wander from my father's face ;
There Absalon, my brother Absalon,
Sweet Absalon shall hear his sister mourn ;
There will I lure with my windy sighs
Night-ravens and owls to rend my bloody side,
Which with a rusty weapon I will wound,
And make them passage to my panting heart.
Why talk'st thou, wretch, and leav'st the deed
     undone ?
Rend hair and garments, as thy heart is rent

With inward fury of a thousand griefs,
And scatter them by these unhallowed doors.

Enter ABSALON.

 ABS. What causeth Thamar to exclaim so
  much?
 THA. The cause that Thamar shameth to dis-
  close.
 ABS. Say; I thy brother will revenge that
  cause.
 THA. Amnon, our father's son, hath forcéd me,
And thrusts me from him as the scorn of Israel.
 ABS. Hath Amnon forcéd thee? by David's
  hand,
And by the covenant God hath made with him,
Amnon shall bear his violence to hell;
Traitor to heaven, traitor to David's throne,
Traitor to Absalon and Israel.
This fact hath Jacob's ruler seen from heaven,
And through a cloud of smoke and tower of fire,
As he rides vaunting him upon the greens,
Shall tear his chariot-wheels with violent winds,
And throw his body in the bloody sea;
At him the thunder shall discharge his bolt;
And his fair spouse, with bright and fiery wings,
Sit ever burning on his hateful bones:

Myself, as swift as thunder or his spouse,
Will hunt occasion with a secret hate,
To work false Amnon an ungracious end.—
Go in, my sister ; rest thee in my house ;
And God in time shall take this shame from thee.

    THA. Nor God nor time will do that good for
      me.   [*Exit.*

Enter DAVID *with his train.*

    DAV. My Absalon, what mak'st thou here alone,
And bear'st such discontentment in thy brows ?

    ABS. Great cause hath Absalon to be displeased,
And in his heart to shroud the wounds of wrath.

    DAV. 'Gainst whom should Absalon be thus dis-
      pleased ?

    ABS. 'Gainst wicked Amnon, thy ungracious
      son,
My brother and fair Thamar's by the king,
My step-brother by mother and by kind :
He hath dishonoured David's holiness,
And fixed a blot of lightness on his throne,
Forcing my sister Thamar when he feigned
A sickness, sprung from root of heinous lust.

    DAV. Hath Amnon brought this evil on my
      house,
And suffered sin to smite his father's bones ?
Smite, David, deadlier than the voice of heaven,

                                    D

And let hate's fire be kindled in thy heart :
Frame in the arches of thy angry brows,
Making thy forehead, like a comet, shine,
To force false Amnon tremble at thy looks.
Sin, with his sevenfold crown and purple robe,
Begins his triumphs in my guilty throne ;
There sits he watching with his hundred eyes
Our idle minutes and our wanton thoughts ;
And with his baits, made of our frail desires,
Gives us the hook that hales our souls to hell :
But with the spirit of my kingdom's God
I'll thrust the flattering tyrant from his throne,
And scourge his bondslaves from my hallowed
      court
With rods of iron and thorns of sharpened steel.
Then, Absalon, revenge not thou this sin ;
Leave it to me, and I will chasten him.
      ABS. I am content : then grant, my lord the
            king,
Himself with all his other lords would come
Up to my sheep-feast on the plain of Hazor.
      DAV. Nay, my fair son, myself with all my
            lords
Will bring thee too much charge ; yet some shall
      go.
      ABS. But let my lord · the king himself take
            pains ;

The time of year is pleasant for your grace,
And gladsome summer in her shady robes,
Crownéd with roses and with painted flowers,
With all her nymphs, shall entertain my lord,
That, from the thicket of my verdant groves,
Will sprinkle honey-dews about his breast,
And cast sweet balm upon his kingly head :
Then grant thy servant's boon, and go, my lord.

DAV. Let it content my sweet son Absalon
That I may stay, and take my other lords.

ABS. But shall thy best-belovéd Amnon go ?

DAV. What needeth it, that Amnon go with
thee ?

ABS. Yet do thy son and servant so much
grace.

DAV. Amnon shall go, and all my other lords,
Because I will give grace to Absalon.

Enter CUSAY *and* URIAS, *with others.*

CU. Pleaseth my lord the king, his servant Joab
Hath sent Urias from the Syrian wars.

DAV. Welcome, Urias, from the Syrian wars,
Welcome to David as his dearest lord.

UR. Thanks be to Israel's God and David's
grace,
Urias finds such greeting with the king.

DAV. No other greeting shall Urias find
As long as David sways th' elected seat
And consecrated throne of Israel.
Tell me, Urias, of my servant Joab ;
Fights he with truth the battles of our God,
And for the honour of the Lord's anointed ?

UR. Thy servant Joab fights the chosen wars
With truth, with honour, and with high success,
And, 'gainst the wicked king of Ammon's sons,
Hath, by the finger of our sovereign's God,
Besieged the city Rabbah, and achieved
The court of waters, where the conduits run,
And all the Ammonites' delightsome springs ;
Therefore he wisheth David's mightiness
Should number out the host of Israel,
And come in person to the city Rabbah,
That so her conquest may be made the king's,
And Joab fight as his inferior.

DAV. This hath not God and Joab's prowess
    done
Without Urias' valour, I am sure,
Who, since his true conversion from a Hethite
To an adopted son of Israel,
Hath fought like one whose arms were lift by
    heaven,
And whose bright sword was edged with Israel's
    wrath.

Go therefore home, Urias, take thy rest ;
Visit thy wife and household with the joys
A victor and a favourite of the king's
Should exercise with honour after arms.

   UR. Thy servant's bones are yet not half so
      crazed,
Nor constitute on such a sickly mould,
That for so little service he should faint,
And seek, as cowards, refuge of his home ;
Nor are his thoughts so sensually stirred,
To stay the arms with which the Lord would
      smite
And fill their circle with his conquered foes,
For wanton bosom of a flattering wife.

   DAV. Urias hath a beauteous sober wife,
Yet young, and framed of tempting flesh and
      blood ;
Then, when the king hath summoned thee from
      arms,
If thou unkindly shouldst withdraw from her,
Sin might be laid upon Urias' soul,
If Bethsabe by frailty hurt her fame :
Then go, Urias, solace in her love ;
Whom God hath knit to thee, tremble to loose.

   UR. The king is much too tender of my ease :
The ark and Israel and Judah dwell
In palaces and rich pavilions ;

But Joab and his brother in the fields,
Suffering the wrath of winter and the sun :
And shall Urias (of more shame than they)
Banquet, and loiter in the work of heaven ?
As sure as thy soul doth live, my lord,
Mine ears shall never lean to such delight,
When holy labour calls me forth to fight.

   DAV. Then be it with Urias' manly heart
As best his fame may shine in Israel.

   UR. Thus shall Urias' heart be best content,
Till thou dismiss me back to Joab's bands :
This ground before the king my master's doors
Shall be my couch, and this unwearied arm
The proper pillow of a soldier's head ;   [*Lies down.*
For never will I lodge within my house,
Till Joab triumph in my secret vows.

   DAV. Then fetch some flagons of our purest
     wine,
That we may welcome home our hardy friend
With full carouses to his fortunes past
And to the honours of his future arms ;
Then will I send him back to Rabbah siege,
And follow with the strength of Israel.

     Enter one with flagons of wine.

Arise, Urias ; come and pledge the king.

UR. If David think me worthy such a grace,
I will be bold and pledge my lord the king.

[*Rises.*

DAV. Absalon and Cusay both shall drink
To good Urias and his happiness.

ABS. We will, my lord, to please Urias' soul.

DAV. I will begin, Urias, to thyself,
And all the treasure of the Ammonites,
Which here I promise to impart to thee,
And bind that promise with a full carouse.

[*Drinks.*

UR. What seemeth pleasant in my sovereign's
eyes,
That shall Urias do till he be dead.

DAV. Fill him the cup.   [URIAS *drinks.*

Follow, ye lords that love
Your sovereign's health, and do as he hath done.

ABS. Ill may he thrive, or live in Israel,
That loves not David, or denies his charge.—
Urias, here is to Abisai's health,
Lord Joab's brother and thy loving friend.

[*Drinks.*

UR. I pledge Lord Absalon and Abisai's health.

[*Drinks.*

CU. Here now, Urias, to the health of Joab,
And to the pleasant journey we shall have
When we return to mighty Rabbah siege. [*Drinks.*

UR. Cusay, I pledge thee all with all my heart.——
Give me some drink, ye servants of the king ;
Give me my drink.   [*Drinks.*

DAV. Well done, my good Urias! drink thy fill,
That in thy fulness David may rejoice.

UR. I will, my lord.

ABS. Now, Lord Urias, one carouse to me.

UR. No, sir, I'll drink to the king ;
Your father is a better man than you.

DAV. Do so, Urias ; I will pledge thee straight.

UR. I will indeed, my lord and sovereign ;
I'll once in my days be so bold.

DAV. Fill him his glass.

UR. Fill me my glass,

DAV. Quickly, I say.

UR. Quickly, I say.——Here, my lord, by your
favour now I drink to you.   [*Drinks.*

DAV. I pledge thee, good Urias, presently.
                                         [*Drinks.*

ABS. Here, then, Urias, once again for me,
And to the health of David's children.   [*Drinks.*

UR. David's children !

ABS. Ay, David's children : wilt thou pledge me,
    man ?

UR. Pledge me, man !

ABS. Pledge me, I say, or else thou lov'st us
    not.

UR. What, do you talk? do you talk? I'll no more ; I'll lie down here.

DAV. Rather, Urias, go thou home and sleep.

UR. O, ho, sir! would you make me break my sentence? [*Lies down.*] Home, sir! no, indeed sir : I'll sleep upon mine arm, like a soldier ; sleep like a man as long as I live in Israel.

DAV. [*aside*]. If naught will serve to save his
 wife's renown,
I'll send him with a letter unto Joab
To put him in the forefront of the wars,
That so my purposes may take effect.—
Help him in, sirs. [*Exeunt* DAVID *and* ABSALON.

CU. Come, rise, Urias ; get thee in and sleep

UR. I will not go home, sir ; that's flat.

CU. Then come and rest thee upon David's bed.

UR. On, afore, my lords, on, afore. [*Exeunt.*

ACT II.

Enter CHORUS.

CHORUS. O proud revolt of a presumptuous man,
Laying his bridle in the neck of sin
Ready to bear him past his grave to hell!
Like as the fatal raven, that in his voice

Carries the dreadful summons of our deaths,
Flies by the fair Arabian spiceries,
Her pleasant gardens and delightsome parks,
Seeming to curse them with his hoarse exclaims,
And yet doth stoop with hungry violence
Upon a piece of hateful carrion ;
So wretched man, displeased with those delights
Would yield a quickening savour to his soul,
Pursues with eager and unstanchéd thirst
The greedy longings of his loathsome flesh.
If holy David so shook hands with sin,
What shall our baser spirits glory in ?
This kingly spirit giving lust her rein
Pursues the sequel with a greater ill.
Urias in the forefront of the wars
Is murdered by the hateful heathens' sword,
And David joys his too dear Bethsabe.
Suppose this past, and that the child is born,
Whose death the prophet solemnly doth mourn.

                                  [*Exit.*

SCENE I.—*Within the Palace of* KING DAVID

Enter BETHSABE *with her* MAID.

BETH. Mourn, Bethsabe, bewail thy foolishness,
Thy sin, thy shame, the sorrow of thy soul :

Sin, shame, and sorrow swarm about thy soul ;
And, in the gates and entrance of my heart,
Sadness, with wreathéd arms, hangs her complaint.
No comfort from the ten-stringed instrument,
The tinkling cymbal, or the ivory lute ;
Nor doth the sound of David's kingly harp
Make glad the broken heart of Bethsabe :
Jerusalem is filled with thy complaint,
And in the streets of Sion sits thy grief.
The babe is sick, sick to the death, I fear,
The fruit that sprung from thee to David's house ;
Nor may the pot of honey and of oil
Glad David or his handmaid's countenance.
Urias—woe is me to think hereon !
For who is it among the sons of men
That saith not to my soul, " The king hath sinned ;
David hath done amiss, and Bethsabe
Laid snares of death unto Urias' life "?
My sweet Urias, fallen into the pit
Art thou, and gone even to the gates of hell
For Bethsabe, that wouldst not shroud her shame.
O, what is it to serve the lust of kings !
How lion-like they rage when we resist !
But, Bethsabe, in humbleness attend   .
The grace that God will to his handmaid send.

                                         [*Exeunt.*

Enter DAVID *in his gown, walking sadly ;*
SERVANTS *attending.*

DAV. [*aside*]. The babe is sick, and sad is David's
    heart,
To see the guiltless bear the guilty's pain.
David, hang up thy harp ; hang down thy head ;
And dash thy ivory lute against the stones !
The dew, that on the hill of Hermon falls,
Rains not on Sion's tops and lofty towers ;
The plains of Gath and Askaron rejoice,
And David's thoughts are spent in pensiveness ;
The babe is sick, sweet babe, that Bethsabe
With woman's pain brought forth to Israel.

Enter NATHAN.

But what saith Nathan to his lord the king ?
    NA. Thus Nathan saith unto his lord the king.
There were two men both dwellers in one town :
The one was mighty, and exceeding rich
In oxen, sheep, and cattle of the field ;
The other poor, having nor ox nor calf,
Nor other cattle, save one little lamb
Which he had bought and nourished by the hand ;
And it grew up, and fed with him and his,

And ate and drank as he and his were wont,
And in his bosom slept, and was to him
As was his daughter or his dearest child.
There came a stranger to this wealthy man ;
And he refused and spared to take his own,
Or of his store to dress or make him meat,
But took the poor man's sheep, the poor man's
    store,
And dressed it for this stranger in his house.
What, tell me, shall be done to him for this ?
    DAV. Now, as the Lord doth live, this wicked
        man
Is judged and shall become the child of death ;
Fourfold to the poor man shall he restore,
That without mercy took his lamb away.
    NA. Thou art the man ; and thou hast judged
        thyself.
David, thus saith the Lord thy God by me :
I thee anointed king in Israel,
And saved thee from the tyranny of Saul ;
Thy master's house I gave thee to possess ;
His wives into thy bosom did I give,
And Judah and Jerusalem withal ;
And might, thou know'st, if this had been too
    small,
Have given thee more :
Wherefore, then, hast thou gone so far astray,

And hast done evil, and sinnéd in my sight?
Urias thou hast killéd with the sword;
Yea, with the sword of the uncircumcised
Thou hast him slain: wherefore, from this day
    forth,
The sword shall never go from thee and thine;
For thou hast ta'en this Hethite's wife to thee:
Wherefore, behold, I will, saith Jacob's God,
In thine own house stir evil up to thee;
Yea, I before thy face will take thy wives,
And give them to thy neighbour to possess:
This shall be done to David in the day,
That Israel openly may see thy shame.

    DAV. Nathan, I have against the Lord, I have
Sinnéd; O, sinnéd grievously! and, lo,
From heaven's throne doth David throw himself,
And groan and grovel to the gates of hell!

                      [Falls down.

    NA. [*raising him*]. David, stand up: thus saith
    the Lord by me:
David the king shall live, for he hath seen
The true repentant sorrow of thy heart;
But, for thou hast in this misdeed of thine
Stirred up the enemies of Israel
To triumph, and blaspheme the God of Hosts,
And say, he set a wicked man to reign
Over his lovéd people and his tribes,—

The child shall surely die, that erst was born,
His mother's sin, his kingly father's scorn.   [*Exit.*

D.AV. How just is Jacob's God in all his works!
But must it die that David loveth so ?
O, that the Mighty One of Israel
Nill change his doom, and says the babe must die!
Mourn, Israel, and weep in Sion-gates ;
Wither, ye cedar-trees of Lebanon ;
Ye sprouting almonds, with your flowering tops,
Droop, drown, and drench in Hebron's fearful streams :
The babe must die that was to David born,
His mother's sin, his kingly father's scorn.

[*Sits sadly.*

Enter CUSAY.

FIRST SERV. What tidings bringeth Cusay to the
    king ?
CU. To thee, the servant of King David's court,
This bringeth Cusay, as the prophet spake ;
The Lord hath surely stricken to the death
The child new-born by that Urias' wife,
That by the sons of Ammon erst was slain.
    FIRST SERV. Cusay, be still ; the king is vexéd
    sore :
How shall he speed that brings this tidings first,
When, while the child was yet alive, we spake,
And David's heart would not be comforted ?

DAV. Yea, David's heart will not be comforted!
What murmur ye, the servants of the king?
What tidings telleth Cusay to the king?
Say, Cusay, lives the child, or is he dead?

CU. The child is dead, that of Urias' wife David
begat.

DAV. Urias' wife, sayest thou?
The child is dead, then ceaseth David's shame:
Fetch me to eat, and give me wine to drink;
Water to wash, and oil to clear my looks;
Bring down your shalms, your cymbals, and your
pipes;
Let David's harp and lute, his hand and voice,
Give laud to Him that loveth Israel,
And sing His praise that shendeth David's fame,
That put away his sin from out His sight,
And sent his shame into the streets of Gath.
Bring ye to me the mother of the babe,
That I may wipe the tears from off her face,
And give her comfort with this hand of mine,
And deck fair Bethsabe with ornaments,
That she may bear to me another son,
That may be lovéd of the Lord of Hosts;
For where he is, of force must David go,
But never may he come where David is.

They bring in water, wine, and oil.   Music and a
banquet ; and enter BETHSABE.

Fair Bethsabe, sit thou, and sigh no more :—
And sing and play, you servants of the king :
Now sleepeth David's sorrow with the dead,
And Bethsabe liveth to Israel.
       [They use all solemnities together and sing, &c.
Now arms and warlike engines for assault
Prepare at once, ye men of Israel,
Ye men of Judah and Jerusalem,
That Rabbah may be taken by the king,
Lest it be calléd after Joab's name,
Nor David's glory shine in Sion streets.
To Rabbah marcheth David with his men,
To chástise Ammon and the wicked ones.

                 [Exeunt.

SCENE II. —*Ammon's Fields on the Plain of Hazor.*   317 wds

1351 letts.

4,26182965

      Enter ABSALON *with several others.*

  ABS. Set up your mules, and give them well to
    eat,
And let us meet our brothers at the feast.
Accurséd is the master of this feast,

Dishonour of the house of Israel,
His sister's slander, and his mother's shame :
Shame be his share that could such ill contrive,
To ravish Thamar, and, without a pause,
To drive her shamefully from out his house :
But may his wickedness find just reward !
Therefore doth Absalon conspire with you,
That Amnon die what time he sits to eat ;
For in the holy temple have I sworn
Wreak of his villany.
And here he comes : bespeak him gently, all,
Whose death is deeply gravéd in my heart.

Enter AMNON, ADONIA, *and* JONADAB.

AM. Our shearers are not far from hence, I wot ;
And Amnon to you all his brethren
Giveth such welcome as our fathers erst
Were wont in Judah and Jerusalem ;—
But, specially, Lord Absalon, to thee,
The honour of thy house and progeny :
Sit down and dine with me, King David's son,
Thou fair young man, whose hairs shine in mine
    eye
Like golden wires of David's ivory lute.
    ABS. Amnon, where be thy shearers and thy
    men,

That we may pour in plenty of thy wines,
And eat thy goats'-milk, and rejoice with thee?
   AM. Here cometh Amnon's shearers and his
      men :—
Absalon, sit and now rejoice with me.

Enter a company of SHEPHERDS, *who dance and sing.*

Drink, Absalon, in praise of Israel;
Welcome to Amnon's fields from David's court.
   ABS. [*stabbing* AMNON]. Die with thy draught;
      perish, and die accursed;
Dishonour to the honour of us all;
Die for the villany to Thamar done,
Unworthy thou to be King David's son!
                    [*Exit with others.*
   JONAD. O, what hath Absalon for Thamar
      done,
Murdered his brother, great King David's son!
   AD. Run, Jonadab, away, and make it known,
What cruelty this Absalon hath shown.
Amnon, thy brother Adonia shall
Bury thy body 'mong the dead men's bones;
And we will make complaint to Israel
Of Amnon's death and pride of Absalon.   [*Exeunt.*

1563 wds.
6527 [lts
4,17 59437

SCENE III.—*The Walls of Rabbah.*

Enter DAVID, JOAB, ABISAI, CUSAY, *and others, with
drum and ensign against Rabbah.*

DAV. This is the town of the uncircumcised,
The city of the kingdom, this is it,
Rabbah, where wicked Hanon sitteth king.
Despoil this king, this Hanon of his crown ;
Unpeople Rabbah and the streets thereof ;
For in their blood, and slaughter of the slain,
Lieth the honour of King David's line.
Joab, Abisai, and the rest of you,
Fight ye this day for great Jerusalem.

Enter HANON *and others on the walls.*

JOAB. And see where Hanon shows him on the
    walls ;
Why, then, do we forbear to give assault,
That Israel may, as it is promiséd,
Subdue the daughters of the Gentiles' tribes ?
All this must be performed by David's hand.
    DAV. Hark to me, Hanon, and remember well :
As sure as He doth live that kept my host
What time our young men, by the pool of Gibeon,

Went forth against the strength of Isboseth,
And twelve to twelve did with their weapons play ;
So sure art thou and all thy men of war
To feel the sword of Israel this day,
Because thou hast defiéd Jacob's God,
And suffered Rabbah with the Philistine
To rail upon the tribe of Benjamin.

    HA. Hark, man : as sure as Saul thy master
       fell,
And gored his sides upon the mountain-tops,
And Jonathan, Abinadab, and Melchisua
Watered the dales and deeps of Askaron
With bloody streams, that from Gilboa ran
In channels through the wilderness of Ziph,
What time the sword of the uncircumcised
Was drunken with the blood of Israel ;
So sure shall David perish with his men,
Under the walls of Rabbah, Hanon's town.

    JOAB. Hanon, the God of Israel hath said,
David the king shall wear that crown of thine
That weighs a talent of the finest gold,
And triumph in the spoil of Hanon's town,
When Israel shall hale thy people hence,
And turn them to the tile-kiln, man and child,
And put them under harrows made of iron,
And hew their bones with axes, and their limbs
With iron swords divide and tear in twain.

Hanon, this shall be done to thee and thine,
Because thou hast defiéd Israel.—
To arms, to arms, that Rabbah feel revenge,
And Hanon's town become King David's spoil !

*Alarum, excursions, assault ; exeunt. Then the trum-
pets sound, and re-enter* DAVID *with* HANON'S
crown, JOAB, *&c.*

   DAV. Now clattering arms and wrathful storms
    of war
Have thundered over Rabbah's razéd towers ;
The wreakful ire of great Jehovah's arm,
That for his people made the gates to rend,
And clothed the cherubins in fiery coats
To fight against the wicked Hanon's town.
Pay thanks, ye men of Judah, to the King,
The God of Sion and Jerusalem,
That hath exalted Israel to this,
And crownéd David with this diadem.
   JOAB. Beauteous and bright is he among the
    tribes ;
As when the sun, attired in glistering robe,
Comes dancing from his oriental gate,
And bridegroom-like hurls through the gloomy air
His radiant beams, such doth King David show,
Crowned with the honour of his enemies' town,

Shining in riches like the firmament,
The starry vault that overhangs the earth ;
So looketh David King of Israel.

   ABIS. Joab, why doth not David mount his
      throne
Whom heaven hath beautified with Hanon's crown ?
Sound trumpets, shalms, and instruments of praise,
To Jacob's God for David's victory. [*Trumpets*, *&c.*

Enter JONADAB.

JONAD. Why doth the King of Israel rejoice ?
Why sitteth David crowned with Rabbah's rule ?
Behold, there hath great heaviness befallen
In Amnon's fields by Absalon's misdeed ;
And Amnon's shearers and their feast of mirth
Absalon hath o'erturnéd with his sword ;
Nor liveth any of King David's sons
To bring this bitter tidings to the king.

   DAV. Ay me, how soon are David's triumphs
      dashed,
How suddenly declineth David's pride !
As doth the daylight settle in the west,
So dim is David's glory and his gite.
Die, David ; for to thee is left no seed
That may revive thy name in Israel.

   JONAD. In Israel is left of David's seed.

Comfort your lord, you servants of the king.—
Behold, thy sons return in mourning weeds,
And only Amnon Absalon hath slain.

Enter ADONIA *with other* SONS *of* DAVID.

DAV. Welcome, my sons ; dearer to me you are
Than is this golden crown or Hanon's spoil.
O, tell me, then, tell me, my sons, I say,
How cometh it to pass that Absalon
Hath slain his brother Amnon with the sword ?
    AD. Thy sons, O king, went up to Amnon's
        fields,
To feast with him and eat his bread and oil ;
And Absalon upon his mule doth come,
And to his men he saith, "When Amnon's heart
Is merry and secure, then strike him dead,
Because he forcéd Thamar shamefully,
And hated her, and threw her forth his doors."
And this did he ; and they with him conspire,
And kill thy son in wreak of Thamar's wrong.
    DAV. How long shall Judah and Jerusalem
Complain, and water Sion with their tears !
How long shall Israel lament in vain,
And not a man among the mighty ones
Will hear the sorrows of King David's heart !
Amnon, thy life was pleasing to thy lord,

As to mine ears the music of my lute,
Or songs that David tuneth to his harp;
And Absalon hath ta'en from me away
The gladness of my sad distressèd soul.

                           [*Exeunt* JOAB *and some others.*

           Enter WOMAN OF THECOA.

   WO. OF T. [*kneeling*]. God save King David, King
     of Israel,
And bless the gates of Sion for his sake!
   DAV. Woman, why mournest thou? rise from
     the earth;
Tell me what sorrow hath befallen thy soul.
   WO. OF T. [*rising*]. Thy servant's soul, O king, is
     troubled sore,
And grievous is the anguish of her heart;
And from Thecoa doth thy handmaid come.
   DAV. Tell me, and say, thou woman of Thecoa,
What aileth thee or what is come to pass.
   WO OF T. Thy servant is a widow in Thecoa.
Two sons thy handmaid had; and they, my lord,
Fought in the field, where no man went betwixt,
And so the one did smite and slay the other.
And, lo, behold, the kindred doth arise,
And cry out upon him that smote his brother,
That he therefore may be the child of death;
" For we will follow and destroy the heir."

So will they quench that sparkle that is left,
And leave nor name nor issue on the earth
To me or to thy handmaid's husband dead.

DAV. Woman, return ; go home unto thy house :
I will take order that thy son be safe.
If any man say otherwise than well,
Bring him to me, and I shall chástise him ;
For, as the Lord doth live, shall not a hair
Shed from thy son or fall upon the earth.
Woman, to God alone belongs revenge :
Shall, then, the kindred slay him for his sin ?

WO. OF T. Well hath King David to his hand-
maid spoke :
But wherefore, then, hast thou determinéd
So hard a part against the righteous tribes,
To follow and pursue the banishéd,
Whenas to God alone belongs revenge ?
Assuredly thou sayest against thyself :
Therefore call home again the banishéd ;
Call home the banishéd, that he may live,
And raise to thee some fruit in Israel.

DAV. Thou woman of Thecoa, answer me,
Answer me one thing I shall ask of thee :
Is not the hand of Joab in this work ?
Tell me, is not his finger in this fact ?

WO. OF T. It is, my lord ; his hand is in this
work ;

Assure thee, Joab, captain of thy host,

Hath put these words into thy handmaid's mouth ;

And thou art as an angel from on high,

To understand the meaning of my heart :

Lo, where he cometh to his lord the king.

Re-enter JOAB.

DAV. Say, Joab, didst thou send this woman in
To put this parable for Absalon ?

JOAB. Joab, my lord, did bid this woman speak,
And she hath said ; and thou hast understood.

DAV. I have, and am content to do the thing.
Go fetch my son, that he may live with me.

JOAB [*kneeling*]. Now God be blessèd for King
David's life !

Thy servant Joab hath found grace with thee,

In that thou sparest Absalon thy child.   [*Rises.*

A beautiful and fair young man is he,

In all his body is no blemish seen ;

His hair is like the wire of David's harp,

That twines about his bright and ivory neck ;

In Israel is not such a goodly man ;

And here I bring him to entreat for grace.

JOAB *brings in* ABSALON.

DAV. Hast thou slain in the fields of Hazor—
Ah, Absalon, my son ! ah, my son, Absalon !

But wherefore do I vex thy spirit so?
Live, and return from Gesur to thy house;
Return from Gesur to Jerusalem:
What boots it to be bitter to thy soul?
Amnon is dead, and Absalon survives.

ABS. Father, I have offended Israel,
I have offended David and his house;
For Thamar's wrong hath Absalon misdone:
But David's heart is free from sharp revenge,
And Joab hath got grace for Absalon.

DAV. Depart with me, you men of Israel,
You that have followed Rabbah with the sword,
And ransack Ammon's richest treasuries.—
Live, Absalon, my son, live once in peace:
Peace be with thee, and with Jerusalem!

[Exeunt all except ABSALON.

ABS. David is gone, and Absalon remains,
Flowering in pleasant spring-time of his youth;
Why liveth Absalon and is not honoured
Of tribes and elders and the mightiest ones,
That round about his temples he may wear
Garlands and wreaths set on with reverence;
That every one that hath a cause to plead
Might come to Absalon and call for right?
Then in the gates of Sion would I sit,
And publish laws in great Jerusalem;
And not a man should live in all the land

But Absalon would do him reason's due :
Therefore I shall address me, as I may,
To love the men and tribes of Israel.   [*Exit.*

ACT III.

1023 wds
4435 ldls.

SCENE I.—*The Tents of* DAVID *by Mount Olivet.*

4.33528837

Enter DAVID, ITHAY, SADOC, AHIMAAS, JONATHAN,
    and others ; DAVID *barefoot,· with some loose
    covering over his head ; and all mourning.*

DAV. Proud lust, the bloodiest traitor to our
    souls,
Whose greedy throat nor earth, air, sea, or heaven
Can glut or satisfy with any store,
Thou art the cause these torments suck my blood,
Piercing with venom of thy poisoned eyes
The strength and marrow of my tainted bones.
To punish Pharaoh and his cursèd host,
The waters shrunk at great Adonai's voice,
And sandy bottom of the sea appeared,
Offering his service at his servant's feet ;
And, to inflict a plague on David's sin,
He makes his bowels traitors to his breast,
Winding about his heart with mortal gripes.

Ah, Absalon, the wrath of heaven inflames
Thy scorchéd bosom with ambitious heat,
And Satan sets thee on a lofty tower,
Showing thy thoughts the pride of Israel,
Of choice to cast thee on her ruthless stones !
Weep with me, then, ye sons of Israel ;
Lie down with David, and with David mourn
Before the Holy One that sees our hearts ;

               [*Lies down and all the rest after him.*

Season this heavy soil with showers of tears,
And fill the face of every flower with dew ;
Weep, Israel, for David's soul dissolves,
Lading the fountains of his drownéd eyes,
And pours her substance on the senseless earth.

  SA. Weep, Israel ; O, weep for David's soul,
Strewing the ground with hair and garments torn,
For tragic witness of your hearty woes !

    AHI. O, would our eyes were conduits to our
      hearts,
And that our hearts were seas of liquid blood,
To pour in streams upon this holy mount,
For witness we would die for David's woes !

    JONATH. Then should this Mount of Olives seem
      a plain
Drowned with a sea, that with our sighs should
      roar,
And, in the murmur of his mounting waves,

Report our bleeding sorrows to the heavens,
For witness we would die for David's woes.

ITH. Earth cannot weep enough for David's
    woes :
Then weep, you heavens, and, all you clouds,
    dissolve,
That piteous stars may see our miseries,
And drop their golden tears upon the ground,
For witness how they weep for David's woes.

SA. Now let my sovereign raise his prostrate
    bones,
And mourn not as a faithless man would do ;
But be assured that Jacob's righteous God,
That promised never to forsake your throne,
Will still be just and pure in his vows.

DAV. Sadoc, high-priest, preserver of the ark,
Whose sacred virtue keeps the chosen crown,
I know my God is spotless in his vows,
And that these hairs shall greet my grave in
    peace :
But that my son should wrong his tendered soul,
And fight against his father's happiness,
Turns all my hopes into despair of him,
And that despair feeds all my veins with grief.

ITH. Think of it, David, as a fatal plague
Which grief preserveth, but preventeth not ;
And turn thy drooping eyes upon the troops

That, of affection to thy worthiness,
Do swarm about the person of the king :
Cherish their valours and their zealous loves
With pleasant looks and sweet encouragements.

    DAV. Methinks the voice of Ithay fills mine
        ears.

    ITH. Let not the voice of Ithay loathe thine
        ears,

Whose heart would balm thy bosom with his
        tears.

    DAV. But wherefore go'st thou to the wars
        with us ?

Thou art a stranger here in Israel,
And son to Achis, mighty King of Gath;
Therefore return, and with thy father stay :
Thou cam'st but yesterday ; and should I now
Let thee partake these troubles here with us ?
Keep both thyself and all thy soldiers safe :
Let me abide the hazards of these arms,
And God requite the friendship thou hast showed.

    ITH. As sure as Israel's God gives David life,
What place of peril shall contain the king
The same will Ithay share in life and death.

    DAV. Then, gentle Ithay, be thou still with us,
A joy to David, and a grace to Israel.—
Go, Sadoc, now, and bear the ark of God
Into the great Jerusalem again :

If I find favour in His gracious eyes,
Then will He lay His hand upon my heart
Yet once again before I visit death ;
Giving it strength, and virtue to mine eyes,
To taste the comforts and behold the form
Of His fair ark and holy tabernacle :
But, if He say, " My wonted love is worn,
And I have no delight in David now,"
Here lie I arméd with an humble heart
T' embrace the pains that anger shall impose,
And kiss the sword my lord shall kill me with.
Then, Sadoc, take Ahimaas thy son,
With Jonathan son to Abiathar ;
And in these fields will I repose myself
Till they return from you some certain news.

SA. Thy servants will with joy obey the king,
And hope to cheer his heart with happy news.

[*Exeunt* SADOC, AHIMAAS, *and* JONATHAN.

ITH. Now that it be no grief unto the king,
Let me for good inform his majesty,
That, with unkind and graceless Absalon,
Achitophel your ancient counsellor
Directs the state of this rebellion.

DAV. Then doth it aim with danger at my
    crown.——
O thou, that hold'st his raging bloody bound
Within the circle of the silver moon,

E

That girds earth's centre with his watery scarf,
Limit the counsel of Achitophel,
No bounds extending to my soul's distress,
But turn his wisdom into foolishness !

Enter CUSAY *with his coat turned and head covered.*

   Cu. Happiness and honour to my lord the
     king !
  Dav. What happiness or honour may betide
His state that toils in my extremities ?
   Cu. O, let my gracious sovereign cease these
     griefs,
Unless he wish his servant Cusay's death,
Whose life depends upon my lord's relief!
Then let my presence with my sighs perfume
The pleasant closet of my sovereign's soul.
  Dav. No, Cusay, no ; thy presence unto me
Will be a burden, since I tender thee,
And cannot brook thy sighs for David's sake :
But if thou turn to fair Jerusalem,
And say to Absalon, as thou hast been
A trusty friend unto his father's seat,
So thou wilt be to him, and call him king,
Achitophel's counsel may be brought to naught.
Then having Sadoc and Abiathar,
All three may learn the secrets of my son,

Sending the message by Ahimaas,
And friendly Jonathan, who both are there.

CU. Then rise, referring the success to heaven.

DAV. Cusay, I rise; though with unwieldy
bones

I carry arms against my Absalon.   [*Exeunt.*

1241 wds
5443 Lers.
4,38597905

SCENE II.—*Within the Palace of* KING DAVID.

ABSALON, AMASA, ACHITOPHEL, *with the* CONCU-
BINES *of* DAVID, *and others, are discovered in
great state ;* ABSALON *crowned.*

ABS. Now you that were my father's concubines,

Have seen his honour shaken in his house,
Which I possess in sight of all the world ;
I bring ye forth for foils to my renown,
And to eclipse the glory of your king,
Whose life is with his honour fast enclosed
Within the entrails of a jetty cloud,
Whose dissolution shall pour down in showers
The substance of his life and swelling pride :
Then shall the stars light earth with rich aspects,
And heaven shall burn in love with Absalon,
Whose beauty will suffice to chase all mists,
And clothe the sun's sphere with a triple fire,

E 2

Sooner than his clear eyes should suffer stain,
Or be offended with a lowering day.

FIRST CONC. Thy father's honour, graceless
    Absalon,
And ours thus beaten with thy violent arms,
Will cry for vengeance to the host of heaven,
Whose power is ever armed against the proud,
And will dart plagues at thy aspiring head
For doing this disgrace to David's throne.

SECOND CONC. To David's throne, to David's
    holy throne,
Whose sceptre angels guard with swords of fire,
And sit as eagles on his conquering fist,
Ready to prey upon his enemies :
Then think not thou, the captain of his foes,
Wert thou much swifter than Azahel * was,
That could outpace the nimble-footed roe,
To scape the fury of their thumping beaks
Or dreadful scope of their commanding wings.

ACH. Let not my lord the King of Israel
Be angry with a silly woman's threats ;
But, with the pleasure he hath erst enjoyed,
Turn them into their cabinets again,
Till David's conquest be their overthrow.

---

* " And there were three sons of Zeruiah there, Joab, and Abishai,
and Asahel : and Asahel was as light of foot as a wild roe."—
2 Samuel ii. 18.

ABS. Into your bowers, ye daughters of disdain,
Gotten by fury of unbridled lust,
And wash your couches with your mourning tears,
For grief that David's kingdom is decayed.

FIRST CONC. No, Absalon, his kingdom is en-
    chained
Fast to the finger of great Jacob's God,
Which will not loose it for a rebel's love.

[*Exeunt* CONCUBINES.

AMA. If I might give advice unto the king,
These concubines should buy their taunts with
    blood.

ABS. Amasa, no ; but let thy martial sword
Empty the veins of David's arméd men,
And let these foolish women scape our hands
To recompense the shame they have sustained.
First, Absalon was by the trumpet's sound
Proclaimed through Hebron King of Israel ;
And now is set in fair Jerusalem
With cómplete state and glory of a crown :
Fifty fair footmen by my chariot run,
And to the air whose rupture rings my fame,
Where'er I ride, they offer reverence.
Why should not Absalon, that in his face
Carries the final purpose of his God,
That is, to work him grace in Israel,
Endeavour to achieve with all his strength

The state that most may satisfy his joy,
Keeping his statutes and his covenants pure ?
His thunder is entangled in my hair,
And with my beauty is his lightning quenched :
I am the man he made to glory in,
When by the errors of my father's sin
He lost the path that led into the land
Wherewith our chosen ancestors were blessed.

Enter CUSAY.

CU. Long may the beauteous King of Israel
    live,
To whom the people do by thousands swarm !
    ABS. What meaneth Cusay so to greet his
    foe ?
Is this the love thou show'st to David's soul,
To whose assistance thou hast vowed thy life ?
Why leav'st thou him in this extremity ?
    CU. Because the Lord and Israel chooseth
    thee ;
And as before I served thy father's turn
With counsel acceptable in his sight,
So likewise will I now obey his son.
    ABS. Then welcome, Cusay, to King Absalon.—
And now, my lords and loving counsellors,
I think it time to exercise our arms

Against forsaken David and his host.
Give counsel first, my good Achitophel,
What times and orders we may best observe
For prosperous manage of these high exploits.

   ACH. Let me choose out twelve thousand valiant
     men :
And, while the night hides with her sable mists
The close endeavours cunning soldiers use,
I will assault thy discontented sire ;
And, while with weakness of their weary arms,
Surcharged with toil, to shun thy sudden power,
The people fly in huge disordered troops
To save their lives, and leave the king alone,
Then will I smite him with his latest wound,
And bring the people to thy feet in peace.

   ABS. Well hath Achitophel given his advice.
Yet let us hear what Cusay counsels us,
Whose great experience is well worth the ear.

   CU. Though wise Achitophel be much more
     meet
To purchase hearing with my lord the king,
For all his former counsels, than myself,
Yet, not offending Absalon or him,
This time it is not good nor worth pursuit ;
For, well thou know'st, thy father's men are
     strong,
Chafing as she-bears robbèd of their whelps :

Besides, the king himself a valiant man,
Trained up in feats and stratagems of war ;
And will not, for prevention of the worst,
Lodge with the common soldiers in the field ;
But now, I know, his wonted policies
Have taught him lurk within some secret cave,
Guarded with all his stoutest soldiers ;
Which, if the forefront of his battle faint,
Will yet give out that Absalon doth fly,
And so thy soldiers be discouragéd :
David himself withal, whose angry heart
Is as a lion's letted of his walk,
Will fight himself, and all his men to one,
Before a few shall vanquish him by fear.
My counsel therefore is, with trumpet's sound
To gather men from Dan to Bersabe,
That they may march in number like sea-sands,
That nestle close in one another's neck :
So shall we come upon him in our strength,
Like to the dew that falls in showers from heaven,
And leave him not a man to march withal.
Besides, if any city succour him,
The numbers of our men shall fetch us ropes,
And we will pull it down the river's stream,
That not a stone be left to keep us out.

    ABS. What says my lord to Cusay's counsel
      now ?

AMA. I fancy Cusay's counsel better far
Than that is given us from Achitophel ;
And so, I think, doth every soldier here.

ALL. Cusay's counsel is better than Achitophel's.

ABS. Then march we after Cusay's counsel all :
Sound trumpets through the bounds of Israel,
And muster all the men will serve the king,
That Absalon may glut his longing soul
With sole fruition of his father's crown.

ACH. [*aside*]. Ill shall they fare that follow thy
    attempts,
That scorns the counsel of Achitophel.

[*Exeunt all except* CUSAY.

CU. Thus hath the power of Jacob's jealous God
Fulfilled his servant David's drifts by me,
And brought Achitophel's advice to scorn.

Enter SADOC, ABIATHAR, AHIMAAS, *and*
    JONATHAN.

SA. God save Lord Cusay, and direct his zeal
To purchase David's conquest 'gainst his son !

ABI. What secrets hast thou gleaned from
    Absalon ?

CU. These, sacred priests that bear the ark of
    God :
Achitophel advised him in the night

To let him choose twelve thousand fighting men,
And he would come on David at unwares,
While he was weary with his violent toil :
But I advised to get a greater host,
And gather men from Dan to Bersabe,
To come upon him strongly in the fields.
Then send Ahimaas and Jonathan
To signify these secrets to the king,
And will him not to stay this night abroad ;
But get him over Jordan presently,
Lest he and all his people kiss the sword.

SA. Then go, Ahimaas and Jonathan,
And straight convey this message to the king.

AHI. Father, we will, if Absalon's chief spies
Prevent not this device, and stay us here.

[*Exeunt.*

SCENE III.—*The Tents of* DAVID *by Mount Olivet.*

Enter SEMEI.

SEM. The man of Israel that hath ruled as
    king,
Or rather as the tyrant of the land,
Bolstering his hateful head upon the throne
That God unworthily hath blessed him with,
Shall now, I hope, lay it as low as hell,

And be deposed from his detested chair.
O, that my bosom could by nature bear
A sea of poison, to be poured upon
His cursèd head that sacred balm hath graced
And consecrated King of Israel!
Or would my breath were made the smoke of hell,
Infected with the sighs of damnèd souls,
Or with the reeking of that serpent's gorge
That feeds on adders, toads, and venomous roots,
That, as I opened my revenging lips
To curse the shepherd for his tyranny,
My words might cast rank poison to his pores,
And make his swoln and rankling sinews crack,
Like to the combat-blows that break the clouds
When Jove's stout champions fight with fire.
See where he cometh that my soul abhors!
I have prepared my pocket full of stones
To cast at him, mingled with earth and dust,
Which, bursting with disdain, I greet him with.

Enter DAVID, JOAB, ABISAI, ITHAY, *and others.*

Come forth, thou murderer and wicked man :
The Lord hath brought upon thy cursèd head
The guiltless blood of Saul and all his sons,
Whose royal throne thy baseness hath usurped ;
And, to revenge it deeply on thy soul,

The Lord hath given the kingdom to thy son,
And he shall wreak the traitorous wrongs of Saul :
Even as thy sin hath still importuned heaven,
So shall thy murders and adultery
Be punished in the sight of Israel,
As thou deserv'st, with blood, with death, and
      hell.
Hence, murderer, hence !

                [*Throws stones and earth at* DAVID.

  ABIS. Why doth this dead dog curse my lord
      the king ?
Let me alone to take away his head.

  DAV. Why meddleth thus the son of Zeruia
To interrupt the action of our God ?
Semei useth me with this reproach
Because the Lord hath sent him to reprove
The sins of David, printed in his brows
With blood that blusheth for his conscience' guilt ;
Who dares, then, ask him why he curseth me ?

   SEM. If, then, thy conscience tell thee thou hast
      sinned,
And that thy life is odious to the world,
Command thy followers to shun thy face :
And by thyself here make away thy soul,
That I may stand and glory in thy shame.

  DAV. I am not desperate, Semei, like thyself,
But trust unto the covenant of my God,

Founded on mercy, with repentance built,
And finished with the glory of my soul.

   SEM. A murderer, and hope for mercy in thy
      end !
Hate and destruction sit upon thy brows
To watch the issue of thy damnéd ghost,
Which with thy latest gasp they'll take and tear,
Hurling in every pain of hell a piece.
Hence, murderer, thou shame to Israel,
Foul lecher, drunkard, plague to heaven and earth !

                  [*Throws again at* DAVID.

   JOAB. What, is it piety in David's thoughts,
So to abhor from laws of policy
In this extremity of his distress,
To give his subjects cause of carelessness ?
Send hence the dog with sorrow to his grave.

   DAV. Why should the sons of Zeruia seek to
      check
His spirit, which the Lord hath thus inspired ? .
Behold, my son which issued from my flesh,
With equal fury seeks to take my life :
How much more then the son of Jemini,
Chiefly since he doth naught but God's com-
      mand ?
It may be, he will look on me this day
With gracious eyes, and for his cursing bless
The heart of David in his bitterness.

SEM. What, dost thou fret my soul with suffer-
   ance ?
O, that the souls of Isboseth and Abner,
Which thou sent'st swimming to their graves in
   blood,
With wounds fresh bleeding, gasping for revenge,
Were here to execute my burning hate !
But I will hunt thy foot with curses still :
Hence, monster, murderer, mirror of contempt !

                    [*Throws again at* DAVID.

Enter AHIMAAS *and* JONATHAN.

AHI. Long life to David, to his enemies death !
DAV. Welcome, Ahimaas and Jonathan :
What news sends Cusay to thy lord the king ?
   AHI. Cusay says he would wish my lord the king
To pass the river Jordan presently,
Lest he and all his people perish here ;
For wise Achitophel hath counselled Absalon
To take advantage of your weary arms,
And come this night upon you in the fields.
But yet the Lord hath made his counsel scorn,
And Cusay's policy with praise preferred ;
Which was to number every Israelite,
And so assault you in their pride of strength.
   JONATH. Abiathar besides entreats the king

To send his men of war against his son,
And hazard not his person in the field.

DAV. Thanks to Abiathar, and to you both,
And to my Cusay, whom the Lord requite ;
But ten times treble thanks to his soft hand
Whose pleasant touch hath made my heart to
    dance
And play him praises in my zealous breast,
That turned the counsel of Achitophel
After the prayers of his servant's lips.
Now will we pass the river all this night,
And in the morning sound the voice of war,
The voice of bloody and unkindly war.

JOAB. Then tell us how thou wilt divide thy
    men,
And who shall have the special charge herein.

DAV. Joab, thyself shall for thy charge conduct
The first third part of all my valiant men ;
The second shall Abisai's valour lead ;
The third fair Ithay, which I most should grace
For comfort he hath done to David's woes ;
And I myself will follow in the midst.

ITH. That let not David ; for, though we should
    fly,
Ten thousand of us were not half so much
Esteemed with David's enemies as himself :
Thy people, loving thee, deny thee this.

DAV. What seems them best, then, that will
    David do.
But now, my lords and captains, hear his voice
That never yet pierced piteous heaven in vain ;
Then let it not slip lightly through your ears :—
For my sake spare the young man Absalon.
Joab, thyself didst once use friendly words
To reconcile my heart incensed to him ;
If, then, thy love be to thy kinsman sound,
And thou wilt prove a perfect Israelite,
Friend him with deeds, and touch no hair of him,—
Not that fair hair with which the wanton winds
Delight to play, and love to make it curl,
Wherein the nightingales would build their nests,
And make sweet bowers in every golden tress
To sing their lover every night asleep :
O, spoil not, Joab, Jove's fair ornaments,
Which he hath sent to solace David's soul !
The best, ye see, my lords, are swift to sin ;
To sin our feet are washed with milk of roes,
And dried again with coals of lightning.
O Lord, thou seest the proudest sin's poor slave,
And with his bridle pull'st him to the grave !
For my sake, then, spare lovely Absalon.
    ITII. We will, my lord, for thy sake favour him.
                 [*Exeunt.*

SCENE IV.—*The House of* ACHITOPHEL.

Enter ACHITOPHEL *with a halter.*

ACH. Now hath Achitophel ordered his house,
And taken leave of every pleasure there :
Hereon depend Achitophel's delights,
And in this circle must his life be closed.
The wise Achitophel, whose counsel proved
Ever as sound for fortunate success
As if men asked the oracle of God,
Is now used like the fool of Israel :
Then set thy angry soul upon her wings,
And let her fly into the shade of death ;
And for my death let heaven for ever weep,
Making huge floods upon the land I leave,
To ravish them and all their fairest fruits.
Let all the sighs I breathed for this disgrace,
Hang on my hedges like eternal mists,
As mourning garments for their master's death.
Ope, earth, and take thy miserable son
Into the bowels of thy curséd womb :
Once in a surfeit thou didst spew him forth ;
Now for fell hunger suck him in again,
And be his body poison to thy veins.
And now, thou hellish instrument of heaven,

Once execute th' arrest of Jove's just doom,
And stop his breath that curseth Israel. [*Exit.*

1156 wds
4910 letts

SCENE V.—*The Wood of Ephraim.*

4,247404844 *Enter* ABSALON, *with* AMASA *and the rest of his train.*

ABS. Now for the crown and throne of Israel,
To be confirmed with virtue of my sword,
And writ with David's blood upon the blade !
Now, Jove, let forth the golden firmament,
And look on him, with all thy fiery eyes,
Which thou hast made to give their glories light :
To show thou lov'st the virtue of thy hand,
Let fall a wreath of stars upon my head,
Whose influence may govern Israel
With state exceeding all her other kings.
Fight, lords and captains, that your sovereign's face
May shine in honour brighter than the sun ;
And with the virtue of my beauteous rays
Make this fair land as fruitful as the fields
That with sweet milk and honey overflowed.
God, in the whizzing of a pleasant wind,
Shall march upon the tops of mulberry-trees,
To cool all breasts that burn with any griefs,

As whilom he was good to Moses' men.
By day the Lord shall sit within a cloud,
To guide your footsteps to the fields of joy;
And in the night a pillar, bright as fire,
Shall go before you, like a second sun,
Wherein the essence of his godhead is;
That day and night you may be brought to peace,
And never swerve from that delightsome path
That leads your souls to perfect happiness.
This shall he do for joy when I am king.
Then fight, brave captains, that these joys may fly
Into your bosoms with sweet victory.   [*Exeunt.*

       [*The battle ; and then* ABSÀLON *hangs by
        the hair.*

ABS. What angry angel, sitting in these shades,
Hath laid his cruel hands upon my hair,
And holds my body thus 'twixt heaven and earth ?
Hath Absalon no soldier near his hand
That may untwine me this unpleasant curl,
Or wound this tree that ravisheth his lord ?
O God, behold the glory of thy hand,
And choicest fruit of Nature's workmanship
Hang, like a rotten branch, upon this tree,
Fit for the axe and ready for the fire !
Since thou withhold'st all ordinary help
To loose my body from this bond of death,
O, let my beauty fill these senseless plants

With sense and power to loose me from this
  plague,
And work some wonder to prevent his death
Whose life thou mad'st a special miracle !

Enter JOAB *with a* SOLDIER.

SOLD. My lord, I saw the young Prince Absalon
Hang by the hair upon a shady oak,
And could by no means get himself unloosed.

JOAB. Why slew'st thou not the wicked Absalon,
That rebel to his father and to heaven,
That so I might have given thee for thy pains
Ten silver shekels and a golden waist ?

SOLD. Not for a thousand shekels would I
  slay
The son of David, whom his father charged
Nor thou, Abisai, nor the son of Gath,
Should touch with stroke of deadly violence.
The charge was given in hearing of us all :
And, had I done it, then, I know, thyself,
Before thou wouldst abide the king's rebuke,
Wouldst have accused me as a man of death.

JOAB. I must not now stand trifling here with
  thee.

ABS. Help, Joab, help, O help thy Absalon !
Let not thy angry thoughts be laid in blood,

In blood of him that sometimes nourished thee,
And softened thy sweet heart with friendly love :
O give me once again my father's sight,
My dearest father and my princely sovereign !
That, shedding tears of blood before his face,
The ground may witness, and the heavens record,
My last submission sound and full of ruth.

    JOAB. Rebel to nature, hate to heaven and
        earth !
Shall I give help to him that thirsts the soul
Of his dear father and my sovereign lord ?
Now see, the Lord hath tangled in a tree
The health and glory of thy stubborn heart,
And made thy pride curbed with a senseless
        plant :
Now, Absalon, how doth the Lord regard
The beauty whereupon thy hope was built,
And which thou thought'st his grace did glory in ?
Find'st thou not now, with fear of instant death,
That God affects not any painted shape
Or goodly personage, when the virtuous soul
Is stuffed with naught but pride and stubborn-
        ness ?
But, preach I to thee, while I should revenge
Thy curséd sin that staineth Israel,
And makes her fields blush with her children's
        blood ?

Take that as part of thy deservéd plague,
Which worthily no torment can inflict. [*Stabs him.*

ABS. O Joab, Joab, cruel, ruthless Joab!
Herewith thou wound'st thy kingly sovereign's
        heart,
Whose heavenly temper hates his children's blood,
Aud will be sick, I know, for Absalon.
O, my dear father, that thy melting eyes
Might pierce this thicket to behold thy son,
Thy dearest son, gored with a mortal dart!
Yet, Joab, pity me : pity my father, Joab ;
Pity his soul's distress that mourns my life,
And will be dead, I know, to hear my death.

JOAB. If he were so remorseful of thy state,
Why sent he me against thee with the sword?
All Joab means to pleasure thee withal
Is, to despatch thee quickly of thy pain :
Hold, Absalon, Joab's pity is in this ;
In this, proud Absalon, is Joab's love.

        [*Stabs him again; and then exit with*
        SOLDIER.

ABS. Such love, such pity Israel's God send
        thee,
And for his love to David pity me!
Ah, my dear father, see thy bowels bleed ;
See death assault thy dearest Absalon ;
See, pity, pardon, pray for Absalon!

Enter five or six SOLDIERS.

FIRST SOLD. See where the rebel in his glory
    hangs.—
Where is the virtue of thy beauty, Absalon ?
Will any of us here now fear thy looks,
Or be in love with that thy golden hair
Wherein was wrapt rebellion 'gainst thy sire,
And cords prepared to stop thy father's breath ?
Our captain Joab hath begun to us ;
And here's an end to thee and all thy sins.
                    [*They stab* ABSALON ; *who dies.*
Come, let us take the beauteous rebel down,
And in some ditch, amidst this darksome wood,
Bury his bulk beneath a heap of stones,
Whose stony heart did hunt his father's death.

Re-enter, in triumph with drum and ensign, JOAB ;
        ABISAI *and* SOLDIERS.

JOAB. Well done, tall soldiers ! take the traitor
    down,
And in this miry ditch inter his bones,
Covering his hateful breast with heaps of stones.
This shady thicket of dark Ephraim
Shall ever lower on his curséd grave ;

Night-ravens and owls shall ring his fatal knell,
And sit exclaiming on his damnéd soul ;
There shall they heap their preys of carrion,
Till all his grave be clad with stinking bones,
That it may loathe the sense of every man :
So shall his end breed horror to his name,
And to his traitorous fact eternal shame.   [*Exeunt.*

Enter CHORUS.

   CHORUS. O dreadful precedent of his just
      doom,
Whose holy heart is never touched with ruth
Of fickle beauty or of glorious shape,
But with the virtue of an upright soul,
Humble and zealous in his inward thoughts,
Though in his person loathsome and deformed !
Now, since this story lends us other store,
To make a third discourse of David's life,
Adding thereto his most renownéd death,
And all their deaths that at his death he judged,
Here end we this, and what here wants to please,
We will supply with treble willingness.   [*Exit.*

ACT IV.

SCENE I.—*The Field of Battle.*

Trumpets sound.   Enter JOAB, AHIMAAS, CUSAY ;
AMASA, *with all the other followers of* ABSALON.

JOAB. Soldiers of Israel, and ye sons of Judah,
That have contended in these irksome broils,
And ript old Israel's bowels with your swords ;
The godless general of your stubborn arms
Is brought by Israel's helper to the grave,
A grave of shame and scorn of all the tribes :
Now, then, to save your honours from the dust,
And keep your bloods in temper by your bones,
Let Joab's ensign shroud your manly heads,
Direct your eyes, your weapons, and your hearts,
To guard the life of David from his foes.
Error hath masked your much-too-forward minds,
And you have sinned against the chosen state,
Against his life, for whom your lives are blessed,
And followed an usurper to the field ;
In whose just death your deaths are threatenéd ;
But Joab pities your disordered souls,
And therefore offers pardon, peace, and love,
To all that will be friendly reconciled

To Israel's weal, to David, and to heaven.
Amasa, thou art leader of the host
That under Absalon have raised their arms ;
Then be a captain wise and politic,
Careful and loving for thy soldiers' lives,
And lead them to this honourable league.

AMA. I will do so ; at least, I'll do my best :
And for the gracious offer thou hast made
I give thee thanks, as much as for my head.—
Then, you deceived poor souls of Israel,
Since now ye see the errors you incurred,
With thanks and due submission be appeased ;
And as ye see your captain's precedent,
Here cast we, then, our swords at Joab's feet,
Submitting with all zeal and reverence
Our goods and bodies to his gracious hands.

                [Kneels with others.

JOAB. Stand up, and take ye all your swords
    again :   *[All stand up.*
David and Joab shall be blessed herein.

AHI. Now let me go inform my lord the king
How God hath freed him from his enemies.

JOAB. Another time, Ahimaas, not now.—
But, Cusay, go thyself, and tell the king
The happy message of our good success.

CU. I will, my lord, and thank thee for thy grace.
                        [Exit.

AIII. What if thy servant should go too, my
lord ?

JOAB. What news hast thou to bring since he is
gone ?

AHI. Yet do Ahimaas so much content,
That he may run about so sweet a charge. `

JOAB. Run, if thou wilt ; and peace be with thy
steps.   [*Exit* AHIMAAS.
Now follow, that you may salute the king
With humble hearts and reconciléd souls.

AMA. We follow, Joab, to our gracious king ;
And him our swords shall honour to our deaths.

[*Exeunt.*

SCENE II.—*King* DAVID'S *Pavilion, by the gates of*
Mahanaim.

Enter DAVID, BETHSABE, SALOMON, NATHAN,
ADONIA, CHILEAB, *with their train.*

BETH. What means my lord, the lamp of Israel,
From whose bright eyes all eyes receive their
light,
To dim the glory of his sweet aspéct,
And paint his countenance with his heart's dis-
tress ?
Why should his thoughts retain a sad conceit,

When every pleasure kneels before his throne,
And sues for sweet acceptance with his grace?
Take but your lute, and make the mountains
    dance,
Retrieve the sun's sphere, and restrain the clouds,
Give ears to trees, make savage lions tame,
Impose still silence to the loudest winds,
And fill the fairest day with foullest storms:
Then why should passions of much meaner power
Bear head against the heart of Israel?
    DAV. Fair Bethsabe, thou mightst increase the
        strength
Of these thy arguments, drawn from my skill,
By urging thy sweet sight to my conceits,
Whose virtue ever served for sacred balm
To cheer my pinings past all earthly joys:
But, Bethsabe, the daughter of the Highest,
Whose beauty builds the towers of Israel,
She that in chains of pearl and unicorn
Leads at her train the ancient golden world,
The world that Adam held in Paradise,
Whose breath refineth all infectious airs,
And makes the meadows smile at her repair,—
She, she, my dearest Bethsabe,
Fair Peace, the goddess of our graces here,
Is fled the streets of fair Jerusalem,
The fields of Israel, and the heart of David,

Leading my comforts in her golden chains,
Linked to the life and soul of Absalon.

   BETH. Then is the pleasure of my sovereign's
     heart
So wrapt within the bosom of that son,
That Salomon, whom Israel's God affects,
And gave the name unto him for his love,
Should be no salve to comfort David's soul ?

   DAV. Salomon, my love, is loved of David's
     lord ;
Our God hath named him lord of Israel :
In him (for that, and since he is thy son)
Must David needs be pleaséd at the heart :
And he shall surely sit upon my throne.
But Absalon, the beauty of my bones,
Fair Absalon, the counterfeit of love,
Sweet Absalon, the image of content,
Must claim a portion in his father's care,
And be in life and death King David's son.

   NATH. Yet, as my lord hath said, let Salomon
     reign,
Whom God in naming hath anointed king.
Now is he apt to learn th' eternal laws,
Whose knowledge being rooted in his youth
Will beautify his age with glorious fruits ;
While Absalon, incensed with graceless pride,
Usurps and stains the kingdom with his sin :

Let Salomon be made thy staff of age,
Fair Israel's rest, and honour of thy race.

    DAV. Tell me, my Salomon, wilt thou embrace
Thy father's precepts gravéd in thy heart,
And satisfy my zeal to thy renown
With practice of such sacred principles
As shall concern the state of Israel ?

    SAL. My royal father, if the heavenly zeal,
Which for my welfare feeds upon your soul,
Were not sustained with virtue of mine own ;
If the sweet accents of your cheerful voice
Should not each hour beat upon mine ears
As sweetly as the breath of heaven to him
That gaspeth scorchéd with the summer's sun,
I should be guilty of unpardoned sin,
Fearing the plague of heaven and shame of earth ;
But since I vow myself to learn the skill
And holy secrets of his mighty hand
Whose cunning tunes the music of my soul,
It would content me, father, first to learn
How the Eternal framed the firmament ;
Which bodies lend their influence by fire,
And which are filled with hoary winter's ice ;
What sign is rainy, and what star is fair ;
Why by the rules of true proportion
The year is still divided into months,
The months to days, the days to certain hours ;

What fruitful race shall fill the future world ;
Or for what time shall this round building stand ;
What magistrates, what kings shall keep in awe
Men's minds with bridles of th' eternal law.

    DAV. Wade not too far, my boy, in waves so deep ;
The feeble eyes of our aspiring thoughts
Behold things present, and record things past ;
But things to come exceed our human reach,
And are not painted yet in angels' eyes :
For those, submit thy sense, and say—" Thou power,
That now art framing of the future world,
Know'st all to come, not by the course of heaven,
By frail conjectures of inferior signs,
By monstrous floods, by flights and flocks of birds,
By bowels of a sacrificéd beast,
Or by the figures of some hidden art ;
But by a true and natural presage,
Laying the ground and perfect architect
Of all our actions now before thine eyes,
From Adam to the end of Adam's seed :
O heaven, protect my weakness with thy strength !
So look on me that I may view thy face,
And see these secrets, written in thy brows.
O sun, come dart thy rays upon my moon !
That now mine eyes, eclipséd to the earth,
May brightly be refined and shine to heaven ;
Transform me from this flesh, that I may live,

Before my death, regenerate with thee.
O thou great God, ravish my earthly sprite!
That for the time a more than human skill
May feed the organons of all my sense;
That, when I think, thy thoughts may be my guide,
And when I speak I may be made by choice
The perfect echo of thy heavenly voice."
Thus say, my son, and thou shalt learn them all.

SAL. A secret fury ravisheth my soul,
Lifting my mind above her human bounds;
And, as the eagle, rouséd from her stand
With violent hunger, towering in the air,
Seizeth her feathered prey, and thinks to feed,
But seeing then a cloud beneath her feet,
Lets fall the fowl, and is emboldenéd
With eyes intentive to bedare the sun,
And styeth close unto his stately sphere;
So Salomon, mounted on the burning wings
Of zeal divine, lets fall his mortal food,
And cheers his senses with celestial air,
Treads in the golden starry labyrinth,
And holds his eyes fixed on Jehovah's brows.
Good father, teach me further what to do.

NATH. See, David, how his haughty spirit mounts,
Even now of height to wield a diadem:
Then make him promise that he may succeed
And rest old Israel's bones from broils of war

DAV. Nathan, thou prophet, sprung from Jesse's
   root,
I promise thee and lovely Bethsabe,
My Salomon shall govern after me.
   BETH. He that hath touched thee with this
      righteous thought
Preserve the harbour of thy thoughts in peace!

Enter MESSENGER.

MESS. My lord, thy servants of the watch have
   seen
One running hitherward from forth the wars.
   DAV. If he be come alone, he bringeth news.
   MESS. Another hath thy servant seen, my lord,
Whose running much resembles Sadoc's son.
   DAV. He is a good man, and good tidings brings.

Enter AHIMAAS.

AHI. Peace and content be with my lord the
   king,
Whom Israel's God hath blessed with victory.
   DAV. Tell me, Ahimaas, lives my Absalon?
   AHI. I saw a troop of soldiers gatheréd,
But know not what the tumult might import.
   DAV. Stand by, until some other may inform
The heart of David with a happy truth.

F

Enter CUSAY.

CU. Happiness and honour live with David's
    soul,
Whom God hath blessed with conquest of his
    foes.
DAV. But, Cusay, lives the young man Absalon?
CU. The stubborn enemies to David's peace,
And all that cast their darts against his crown,
Fare ever like the young man Absalon!
For as he rid the woods of Ephraim,
Which fought for thee as much as all thy men,
His hair was tangled in a shady oak;
And hanging there, by Joab and his men
Sustained the stroke of well-deservéd death.
DAV. Hath Absalon sustained the stroke of
    death?
Die, David, for the death of Absalon,
And make these curséd news the bloody darts
That through his bowels rip thy wretched breast.
Hence, David, walk the solitary woods,
And in some cedar's shade the thunder slew,
And fire from heaven hath made his branches black,
Sit mourning the decease of Absalon:
Against the body of that blasted plant
In thousand shivers break thy ivory lute,

Hanging thy stringless harp upon his boughs ;
And through the hollow sapless sounding trunk
Bellow the torments that perplex thy soul.
There let the winds sit sighing till they burst ;
Let tempest, muffled with a cloud of pitch,
Threaten the forests with her hellish face,
And, mounted fiercely on her iron wings,
Rend up the wretched engine by the roots
That held my dearest Absalon to death.
Then let them toss my broken lute to heaven,
Even to his hands that beats me with the strings,
To show how sadly his poor shepherd sings.

> [*Goes to his pavilion and sits close a while.*

BETH. Die, Bethsabe, to see thy David mourn,
To hear his tunes of anguish and of hell.
O help, my David, help thy Bethsabe,
Whose heart is piercéd with thy breathy swords,
And bursts with burden of ten thousand griefs !

> [*Lies down.*

Now sits thy sorrows sucking of my blood :
O, that it might be poison to their powers,
And that their lips might draw my bosom dry,
So David's love might ease him, though she die !

NATH. These violent passions come not from
    above ;
David and Bethsabe offend the Highest,
To mourn in this immeasurable sort

DAV. [*looking forth*]. O Absalon, Absalon ! O my
  son, my son !
Would God that I had died for Absalon !
But he is dead ; ah, dead !   Absalon is dead :
And David lives to die for Absalon.

                                    [*Sits close again.*

Enter JOAB, ABISAI, ITHAY, *and their train.*

JOAB. Why lies the queen so prostrate on the
  ground ?
Why is this company so tragic-hued ?
Why is the king now absent from his men,
And marcheth not in triumph through the gates ?
                                    [*Unfolds the pavilion.*
David, awake ; if sleep have shut thine eyes,
Sleep of affection, that thou canst not see
The honour offered to the victor's head :
Joab brings conquest piercéd on his spear
And joy from all the tribes of Israel.

  DAV. Thou man of blood, thou sepulchre of death,
Whose marble breast intombs my bowels quick,
Did I not charge thee, nay, entreat thy hand,
Even for my sake, to spare my Absalon ?
And hast thou now, in spite of David's health,
And scorn to do my heart some happiness,
Given him the sword and spilt his purple soul ?

JOAB. What, irks it David, that the victor
    breathes,
That Juda and the fields of Israel
Should cleanse their faces from their children's blood ?
What, art thou weary of thy royal rule ?
Is Israel's throne a serpent in thine eyes,
And he that set thee there so far from thanks,
That thou must curse his servant for his sake ?
Hast thou not said that, as the morning light,
The cloudless morning, so should be thine house,
And not as flowers by the brightest rain
Which grow up quickly and as quickly fade ?
Hast thou not said, the wicked are as thorns,
That cannot be preservéd with the hand,
And that the man shall touch them must be armed
With coats of iron and garments made of steel,
Or with the shaft of a defencéd spear ?
And art thou angry he is now cut off
That led the guiltless swarming to their deaths,
And was more wicked than an host of men ?
Advance thee from thy melancholy den,
And deck thy body with thy blissful robes,
Or, by the lord that sways the heaven I swear,
I'll lead thine armies to another king
Shall cheer them for their princely chivalry,
And not sit daunted, frowning in the dark,
When his fair looks, with oil and wine refreshed,

Should dart into their bosoms gladsome beams,
And fill their stomachs with triumphant feasts
That when elsewhere stern war shall sound his
    trump,
And call another battle to the field,
Fame still may bring thy valiant soldiers home,
And for their service happily confess
She wanted worthy trumps to sound their prowess :
Take thou this course and live ; refuse and die.

    ABIS. Come, brother, let him sit there till he sink ;
Some other shall advance the name of Joab.
                        [Offers to go out with JOAB.
    BETH. [*rising*]. O, stay, my lords, stay ! David
    mourns no more,
But riseth to give honour to your acts.
    DAV. [*rising, and coming from his pavilion*]. Then
    happy art thou, David's fairest son,
That, freéd from the yoke of earthly toils,
And séquestered from sense of human sins,
Thy soul shall joy the sacred cabinet
Of those divine ideas that present
Thy changéd spirit with a heaven of bliss.
Then thou art gone ; ah, thou art gone, my son !
To heaven, I hope, my Absalon is gone :
Thy soul there placed in honour of the saints,
Or angels clad with immortality,
Shall reap a sevenfold grace for all thy griefs ;

Thy eyes, now no more eyes but shining stars,
Shall deck the flaming heavens with novel lamps ;
There shalt thou taste the drink of seraphins,
And cheer thy feelings with archangels' food ;
Thy day of rest, thy holy sabbath-day,
Shall be eternal ; and, the curtain drawn,
Thou shalt behold thy sovereign face to face,
With wonder, knit in triple unity,
Unity infinite and innumerable.—
Courage, brave captains ! Joab's tale hath stirred,
And made the suit of Israel preferred.

JOAB. Bravely resolved. and spoken like a king :
Now may old Israel and his daughters sing.

[*Music.   Exeunt omnes.*

THE OLD WIVES' TALE.

DRAMATIS PERSONÆ.

SACRAPANT.	GHOST OF JACK.
FIRST BROTHER, *named* CALYPHA.	DELIA, *sister to* CALYPHA *and* THELEA.
SECOND BROTHER, *named* THELEA.	VENELIA, *betrothed to* ERESTUS.
EUMENIDES.	ZANTIPPA, | *daughters to* LAM- CELANTA, | PRISCUS.
ERESTUS.	HOSTESS.
LAMPRISCUS.	ANTIC.
HUANEBANGO.	FROLIC.
COREBUS.	FANTASTIC.
WIGGEN.	CLUNCH, *a smith.*
CHURCHWARDEN.	MADGE, *his wife.*
SEXTON.	

Friar, Harvestmen, Furies, Fiddlers, &c.

Enter ANTIC, FROLIC, *and* FANTASTIC.

ANT. How now, fellow Frolic! what, all amort? doth this sadness become thy madness? What though we have lost our way in the woods? yet never hang the head as though thou hadst no hope to live till to-morrow; for Fantastic and I will warrant thy life to-night for twenty in the hundred.

FRO. Antic, and Fantastic, as I am frolic franion,
never in all my life was I so dead slain. What, to
lose our way in the wood, without either fire or
candle, so uncomfortable? *O cœlum! O terra! O
maria!* O Neptune!

FAN. Why makes thou it so strange, seeing Cupid
hath led our young master to the fair lady, and she
is the only saint that he hath sworn to serve?

FRO. What resteth, then, but we commit him to
his saint, and each of us take his stand up in a tree,
and sing out our ill fortune to the tune of "O man
in desperation"?

ANT. Desperately spoken, fellow Frolic, in the
dark: but seeing it falls out thus, let us rehearse the
old proverb:

> "Three merry men, and three merry men,
> And three merry men be we;
> I in the wood, and thou on the ground,
> And Jack sleeps in the tree."

FAN. Hush! a dog in the wood, or a wooden
dog! O comfortable hearing! I had even as lief
the chamberlain of the White Horse had called me
up to bed.

FRO. Either hath this trotting cur gone out of
his circuit, or else are we near some village, which
should not be far off, for I perceive the glimmering

of a glow-worm, a candle, or a cat's eye, my life for a halfpenny!

Enter CLUNCH *with a lantern and candle.*

In the name of my own father, be thou ox or ass that appearest, tell us what thou art.

CLUNCH. What am I! why, I am Clunch the smith. What are you? what make you in my territories at this time of the night?

ANT. What do we make, dost thou ask? why, we make faces for fear.

FRO. And, in faith, sir, unless your hospitality do relieve us, we are like to wander, with a sorrowful heigh-ho, among the owlets and hobgoblins of the forest. Good Vulcan, for Cupid's sake that hath cozened us all, befriend us as thou mayst; and command us howsoever, wheresoever, whensoever, in whatsoever, for ever and ever.

CLUNCH. Well, masters, it seems to me you have lost your way in the wood : in consideration whereof, if you will go with Clunch to his cottage, you shall have house-room and a good fire to sit by, although we have no bedding to put you in.

ALL. O blessed smith, O bountiful Clunch!

CLUNCH. For your further entertainment, it shall be as it may be, so and so. [*A dog barks within.*]

Hark! this is Ball my dog, that bids you all welcome
in his own language : come, take heed for stumbling
on the threshold.—Open door, Madge; take in
guests.

Enter MADGE.

MADGE. Welcome, Clunch, and good fellows all,
that come with my good-man : for my good-man's
sake, come on, sit down : here is a piece of cheese,
and a pudding of my own making.

ANT. Thanks, gammer : a good example for the
wives of our town.

FRO. Gammer, thou and thy good-man sit lov-
ingly together ; we come to chat, and not to eat.

CLUNCH. Well, masters, if you will eat nothing,
take away. Come, what do we to pass away the
time? Lay a crab in the fire to roast for lamb's-
wool. What, shall we have a game at trump or ruff
to drive away the time? How say you?

FAN. This smith leads a life as merry as a king
with Madge his wife. Sirrah Frolic, I am sure thou
art not without some round or other; no doubt but
Clunch can bear his part.

FRO. Else think you me ill brought up : so set to
it when you will.   [*They sing.*

SONG.

Whenas the rye reach to the chin,
And chopcherry, chopcherry ripe within,
Strawberries swimming in the cream,
And school-boys playing in the stream ;
Then, O then, O then, O my true-love said,
Till that time come again
She could not live a maid.

ANT. This sport does well ; but methinks, gammer, a merry winter's tale would drive away the time trimly : come, I am sure you are not without a score.

FAN. I'faith, gammer, a tale of an hour long were as good as an hour's sleep.

FRO. Look you, gammer, of the giant and the king's daughter, and I know not what : I have seen the day, when I was a little one, you might have drawn me a mile after you with such a discourse.

MADGE. Well, since you be so importunate, my good-man shall fill the pot and get him to bed ; they that ply their work must keep good hours : one of you go lie with him ; he is a clean-skinned man I tell you, without either spavin or windgall : so I am content to drive away the time with an old wives' winter's tale.

FAN. No better hay in Devonshire ; o' my word, gammer, I'll be one of your audience.

FRO. And I another, that's flat.

ANT. Then must I to bed with the good-man.— *Bona nox,* gammer.—Good night, Frolic.

CLUNCH. Come on, my lad, thou shalt take thy unnatural rest with me.   [*Exit with* ANTIC.

FRO. Yet this vantage shall we have of them in the morning, to be ready at the sight thereof extempore.

MADGE. Now this bargain, my masters, must I make with you, that you will say hum and ha to my tale, so shall I know you are awake.

BOTH. Content, gammer, that will we do.—

MADGE. Once upon a time, there was a king, or a lord, or a duke, that had a fair daughter, the fairest that ever was ; as white as snow and as red as blood : and once upon a time his daughter was stolen away : and he sent all his men to seek out his daughter ; and he sent so long, that he sent all his men out of his land.

FRO. Who drest his dinner, then ?

MADGE. Nay, either hear my tale, or turn tail.

FAN. Well said ! on with your tale, gammer.

MADGE. O Lord, I quite forgot ! there was a conjurer, and this conjurer could do anything, and

he turned himself into a great dragon, and carried
the king's daughter away in his mouth to a castle
that he made of stone ; and there he kept her I
know not how long, till at last all the king's men
went out so long that her two brothers went to seek
her. O, I forget! she (he, I would say) turned a
proper young man to a bear in the night, and a man
in the day, and keeps by a cross that parts three
several ways ; and he made his lady run mad,—Ods
me bones, who comes here ?

Enter the TWO BROTHERS.

FRO. Soft, gammer, here some come to tell your
    tale for you.
FAN. Let   m alone ; let us hear what they will
    say.
FIRST BRO. Upon these chalky cliffs of Albion
We are arrivéd now with tedious toil ;
And compassing the wide world round about,
To seek our sister, seek fair Delia forth,
Yet cannot we so much as hear of her.
    SECOND BRO. O fortune cruel, cruel and unkind !
Unkind in that we cannot find our sister,
Our sister, hapless in her cruel chance.—
Soft ! who have we here ?

Enter ERESTUS *at the cross, stooping to gather.*

FIRST BRO. Now, father, God be your speed !
what do you gather there ?

EREST. Hips and haws, and sticks and straws,
and things that I gather on the ground, my son.

FIRST BRO. Hips and haws, and sticks and straws !
why, is that all your food, father ?

EREST. Yea, son.

SECOND BRO. Father, here is an alms-penny for
me ; and if I speed in that I go for, I will give thee
as good a gown of grey as ever thou didst wear.

FIRST BRO. And, father, here is another alms-
penny for me ; and if I speed in my journey, I will
give thee a palmer's staff of ivory, and a scallop-shell
of beaten gold.

EREST. Was she fair ?

SECOND BRO. Ay, the fairest for white, and the
purest for red, as the blood of the deer, or the
driven snow.

EREST. Then hark well, and mark well, my old
        spell :
Be not afraid of every stranger ;
Start not aside at every danger ;
Things that seem are not the same ;
Blow a blast at every flame ;

For when one flame of fire goes out,
Then come your wishes well about :
If any ask who told you this good,
Say, the white bear of England's wood.

    FIRST BRO. Brother, heard you not what the old
       man said ?
Be not afraid of every stranger ;
Start not aside for every danger ;
Things that seem are not the same ;
Blow a blast at every flame ;
For when one flame of fire goes out,
Then come your wishes well about :
If any ask who told you this good,
Say, the white bear of England's wood.

    SECOND BRO. Well, if this do us any good,
Well fare the white bear of England's wood !
              [*Exeunt the* TWO BROTHERS.

    ERES. Now sit thee here, and tell a heavy tale,
Sad in thy mood, and sober in thy cheer ;
Here sit thee now, and to thyself relate
The hard mishap of thy most wretched state.
In Thessaly I lived in sweet content,
Until that fortune wrought my overthrow ;
For there I wedded was unto a dame,
That lived in honour, virtue, love, and fame.
But Sacrapant, that cursèd sorcerer,
Being besotted with my beauteous love

My dearest love, my true betrothéd wife,
Did seek the means to rid me of my life.
But worse than this, he with his 'chanting spells
Did turn me straight unto an ugly bear ;
And when the sun doth settle in the west,
Then I begin to don my ugly hide :
And all the day I sit, as now you see,
And speak in riddles, all inspired with rage,
Seeming an old and miserable man,
And yet I am in April of my age.

Enter VENELIA *mad ; and goes in again.*

See where Venelia, my betrothéd love,
Runs madding, all enraged, about the woods,
All by his curséd and enchanting spells.—
But here comes Lampriscus, my discontented
    neighbour.

Enter LAMPRISCUS *with a pot of honey.*

How now, neighbour ! you look towards the ground
as well as I : you muse on something.

LAMP. Neighbour, on nothing but on the matter
I so often moved to you : if you do anything for
charity, help me ; if for neighbourhood or brother-
hood, help me ; never was one so cumbered as is

poor Lampriscus ; and to begin, I pray receive this pot of honey, to mend your fare.

EREST. Thanks, neighbour, set it down ; honey is always welcome to the bear. And now, neighbour, let me hear the cause of your coming.

LAMP. I am, as you know, neighbour, a man un-married, and lived so unquietly with my two wives, that I keep every year holy the day wherein I buried them both : the first was on Saint Andrew's day, the other on Saint Luke's.

EREST. And now, neighbour, you of this country say, your custom is out. But on with your tale, neighbour.

LAMP. By my first wife, whose tongue wearied me alive, and sounded in my ears like the clapper of a great bell, whose talk was a continual torment to all that dwelt by her or lived nigh her, you have heard me say I had a handsome daughter.

EREST. True, neighbour.

LAMP. She it is that afflicts me with her continual clamours, and hangs on me like a bur : poor she is, and proud she is ; as poor as a sheep new-shorn, and as proud of her hopes as a peacock of her tail well-grown.

EREST. Well said, Lampriscus ! you speak it like an Englishman.

LAMP. As curst as a wasp, and as froward as a

child new-taken from the mother's teat ; she is to my age, as smoke to the eyes, or as vinegar to the teeth.

EREST. Holily praised, neighbour. As much for the next.

LAMP. By my other wife I had a daughter so hard-favoured, so foul, and ill faced, that I think a grove full of golden trees, and the leaves of rubies and diamonds, would not be a dowry answerable to her deformity.

EREST. Well, neighbour, now you have spoke, hear me speak : send them to the well for the water of life ; there shall they find their fortunes unlooked for. Neighbour, farewell.

LAMP. Farewell, and a thousand. [*Exit* ERESTUS.] And now goeth poor Lampriscus to put in execution this excellent counsel. [*Exit.*

FRO. Why, this goes round without a fiddling-stick : but, do you hear, gammer, was this the man that was a bear in the night and a man in the day ?

MADGE. Ay, this is he ; and this man that came to him was a beggar, and dwelt upon a green. But soft ! who come here ? O, these are the harvest-men ; ten to one they sing a song of mowing.

Enter the HARVESTMEN *a-singing, with this song double repeated.*

All ye that lovely lovers be,
Pray you for me :
Lo, here we come a-sowing, a-sowing,
And sow sweet fruits of love ;
In your sweet hearts well may it prove!

[*Exeunt.*

Enter HUANEBANGO *with his two-hand sword, and* COREBUS.

FAN. Gammer, what is he ?

MADGE. O, this is one that is going to the conjurer : let him alone, hear what he says.

HUAN. Now, by Mars and Mercury, Jupiter and Janus, Sol and Saturnus, Venus and Vesta, Pallas and Proserpina, and by the honour of my house, Polimackeroeplacidus, it is a wonder to see what this love will make silly fellows adventure, even in the wane of their wits and infancy of their discretion. Alas, my friend, what fortune calls thee forth to seek thy fortune among brazen gates, enchanted towers, fire and brimstone, thunder and lightning ? Her beauty, I tell thee, is peerless, and she precious whom thou affectest. Do off these desires, good countryman : good friend, run away from thyself ; and, so soon as thou canst, forget her, whom none must inherit but he that can monsters tame, labours achieve, riddles absolve, loose enchantments, murder magic, and kill conjuring,—and that is the great and mighty Huanebango.

COR. Hark you, sir, hark you. First know I have here the flurting feather, and have given the parish the start for the long stock : now, sir, if it be no more but running through a little lightning and thunder, and " riddle me, riddle me what's this ? " I'll have the wench from the conjurer, if he were ten conjurers.

HUAN. I have abandoned the court and honourable company, to do my devoir against this sore sorcerer and mighty magician : if this lady be so fair as she is said to be, she is mine, she is mine ; *meus, mea, meum, in contemptum omnium grammaticorum.*

COR. *O falsum Latinum !*
The fair maid is *minum,*
Cum apurtinantibus gibletis and all.

HUAN. If she be mine, as I assure myself the heavens will do somewhat to reward my worthiness, she shall be allied to none of the meanest gods, but be invested in the most famous stock of Huanebango, —Polimackeroeplacidus my grandfather, my father

Pergopolineo, my mother Dionora de Sardinia, famously descended.

COR. Do you hear, sir? had not you a cousin that was called Gusteceridis?

HUAN. Indeed, I had a cousin that sometime followed the court infortunately, and his name Bustegusteceridis.

COR. O Lord, I know him well! he is the knight of the neat's-feet.

HUAN. O, he loved no capon better! he hath oftentimes deceived his boy of his dinner; that was his fault, good Bustegusteceridis.

COR. Come, shall we go along?

Enter ERESTUS *at the cross.*

Soft! here is an old man at the cross: let us ask him the way thither.—Ho, you gaffer! I pray you tell where the wise man the conjurer dwells.

HUAN. Where that earthly goddess keepeth her abode, the commander of my thoughts, and fair mistress of my heart.

EREST. Fair enough, and far enough from thy fingering, son.

HUAN. I will follow my fortune after mine own fancy, and do according to mine own discretion.

EREST. Yet give something to an old man before you go.

HUAN. Father, methinks a piece of this cake might serve your turn.

EREST. Yea, son.

HUAN. Huanebango giveth no cakes for alms : ask of them that give gifts for poor beggars.—Fair lady, if thou wert once shrined in this bosom, I would buckler thee haratantara.   [*Exit.*

COR. Father, do you see this man ? you little think he'll run a mile or two for such a cake, or pass for a pudding.   I tell you, father, he has kept such a begging of me for a piece of this cake!   Whoo! he comes upon me with "a superfantial substance, and the foison of the earth," that I know not what he means.   If he came to me thus, and said, "My friend Corebus," or so, why, I could spare him a piece with all my heart ; but when he tells me how God hath enriched me above other fellows with a cake, why, he makes me blind and deaf at once.   Yet, father, here is a piece of cake for you, as hard as the world goes,

                                                [*Gives cake.*

EREST. Thanks, son, but list to me ;
He shall be deaf when thou shalt not see.
Farewell, my son : things may so hit,
Thou mayst have wealth to mend thy wit.

COR. Farewell, father, farewell ; for I must make haste after my two-hand sword that is gone before.

                                        [*Exeunt severally.*

Enter SACRAPANT *in his study.*

SAC. The day is clear, the welkin bright and
grey,
The lark is merry and records her notes ;
Each thing rejoiceth underneath the sky,
But only I, whom heaven hath in hate,
Wretched and miserable Sacrapant.
In Thessaly was I born and brought up :
My mother Meroe hight, a famous witch,
And by her cunning I of her did learn
To change and alter shapes of mortal men.
There did I turn myself into a dragon,
And stole away the daughter to the king,
Fair Delia, the mistress of my heart ;
And brought her hither to revive the man
That seemeth young and pleasant to behold,
And yet is agéd, crookéd, weak, and numb.
Thus by enchanting spells I do deceive
Those that behold and look upon my face ;
But well may I bid youthful years adieu.
See where she comes from whence my sorrows
grow !

Enter DELIA *with a pot in her hand.*

How now, fair Delia ! where have you been ?

DEL. At the foot of the rock for running water, and gathering roots for your dinner, sir.

SAC. Ah, Delia,
Fairer art thou than the running water,
Yet harder far than steel or adamant!

DEL. Will it please you to sit down, sir?

SAC. Ay, Delia, sit and ask me what thou wilt,
Thou shalt have it brought into thy lap.

DEL. Then, I pray you, sir, let me have the best meat from the King of England's table, and the best wine in all France, brought in by the veriest knave in all Spain.

SAC. Delia, I am glad to see you so pleasant:
Well, sit thee down.—

> Spread, table, spread,
> Meat, drink, and bread.
> Ever may I have
> What I ever crave.
> When I am spread,
> Meat for my black cock,
> And meat for my red.

Enter a FRIAR *with a chine of beef and a pot
of wine.*

Here, Delia, will ye fall to?

DEL. Is this the best meat in England?

SAC. Yea.

DEL. What is it?

SAC. A chine of English beef, meat for a king and a king's followers.

DEL. Is this the best wine in France?

SAC. Yea.

DEL. What wine is it?

SAC. A cup of neat wine of Orleans, that never came near the brewers in England.

DEL. Is this the veriest knave in all Spain?

SAC. Yea.

DEL. What, is he a friar?

SAC. Yea, a friar indefinite, and a knave infinite.

DEL. Then, I pray ye, Sir Friar, tell me before you go, which is the most greediest Englishman?

FRI. The miserable and most covetous usurer.

SAC. Hold thee there, friar. [*Exit* FRIAR.] But, soft!

Who have we here?   Delia, away, be gone!

Enter the TWO BROTHERS.

Delia, away! for beset are we.—

But heaven or hell shall rescue her for me.

[*Exeunt* DELIA *and* SACRAPANT.

FIRST BRO. Brother, was not that Delia did appear,

Or was it but her shadow that was here?

SECOND BRO. Sister, where art thou? Delia, come again!

He calls, that of thy absence doth complain.—
Call out, Calypha, so that she may hear,
And cry aloud, for Delia is near.

ECHO. Near.

FIRST BRO. Near! O, where? hast thou any tidings?

ECHO. Tidings.

SECOND BRO. Which way is Delia, then? or that, or this?

ECHO. This.

FIRST BRO. And may we safely come where Delia is?

ECHO. Yes.

SECOND BRO. Brother, remember you the white bear of England's wood?
"Start not aside for every danger,
Be not afeard of every stranger;
Things that seem are not the same."

FIRST BRO. Brother,
Why do we not, then, courageously enter?

SECOND BRO. Then, brother, draw thy sword and follow me.

Re-enter SACRAPANT : *it lightens and thunders ;
the* SECOND BROTHER *falls down.*

FIRST BRO. What, brother, dost thou fall ?
SAC. Ay, and thou too, Calypha.

              [*The* FIRST BROTHER *falls down.*
Adeste, dæmones !

Enter TWO FURIES.

        Away with them :
Carry them straight to Sacrapanto's cell,
There in despair and torture for to dwell.

        [*Exeunt* FURIES *with the* TWO BROTHERS.
These are Thenores' sons of Thessaly,
That come to seek Delia their sister forth ;
But, with a potion I to her have given,
My arts have made her to forget herself.

        [*Removes a turf, and shows a light in a
        glass.*
See here the thing which doth prolong my life,
With this enchantment I do anything ;
And till this fade, my skill shall still endure ;
And never none shall break this little glass,
But she that's neither wife, widow, nor maid :
Then cheer thyself ; this is thy destiny,
Never to die but by a dead man's hand.   [*Exit.*

Enter EUMENIDES.

EUM. Tell me, Time,
Tell me, just Time, when shall I Delia see?
When shall I see the loadstar of my life?
When shall my wandering course end with her
    sight,
Or I but view my hope, my heart's delight?

Enter ERESTUS *at the cross.*

Father, God speed! if you tell fortunes, I pray, good
father, tell me mine.
    EREST. Son, I do see in thy face
Thy blessèd fortune work apace:
I do perceive that thou hast wit;
Beg of thy fate to govern it,
For wisdom governed by advice,
Makes many fortunate and wise.
Bestow thy alms, give more than all,
Till dead men's bones come at thy call.
Farewell, my son: dream of no rest,
Till thou repent that thou didst best.   [*Exit.*
    EUM. This man hath left me in a labyrinth:
He biddeth me give more than all,
Till dead men's bones come at my call;

He biddeth me dream of no rest,
Till I repent that I do best.   [*Lies down and sleeps.*

Enter WIGGEN, COREBUS, CHURCHWARDEN, *and*
SEXTON.

WIG. You may be ashamed, you rascally scal l
Sexton and Churchwarden, if you had any shame in
those shameless faces of yours, to let a poor man lie
so long above ground unburied.   A rot on you all,
that have no more compassion of a good fellow when
he is gone !

CHURCH. What, would you have us to bury him
and to answer it ourselves to the parish ?

SEX. Parish me no parishes ; pay me my fees,
and let the rest run on in the quarter's accounts, and
put it down for one of your good deeds, o' God's
name ! for I am not one that curiously stands upon
merits.

COR. You rascally, sodden-headed sheep's face,
shall a good fellow do less service and more honesty
to the parish, and will you not, when he is dead, let
him have Christmas burial ?

WIG. Peace, Corebus ! as sure as Jack was Jack,
the frolic'st franion amongst you, and I, Wiggen, his
sweet sworn brother, Jack shall have his funerals, or
some of them shall lie on God's dear earth for it,
that's once.

CHURCH, Wiggen, I hope thou wilt do no more than thou darest answer.

WIG. Sir, sir, dare or dare not, more or less, answer or not answer,—do this, or have this.

SEX. Help, help, help!

> [WIGGEN *sets upon the parish with a pike-staff:* EUMENIDES *awakes and comes to them.*

EUM. Hold thy hands, good fellow.

COR. Can you blame him, sir, if he take Jack's part against this shake-rotten parish that will not bury Jack?

EUM. Why, what was that Jack?

COR. Who, Jack, sir? who, our Jack, sir? as good a fellow as ever trod upon neat's-leather.

WIG. Look you, sir; he gave fourscore and nineteen mourning gowns to the parish, when he died, and because he would not make them up a full hundred, they would not bury him: was not this good dealing?

CHURCH. O Lord, sir, how he lies! he was not worth a halfpenny, and drunk out every penny; and now his fellows, his drunken companions, would have us to bury him at the charge of the parish. An we make many such matches, we may pull down the steeple, sell the bells, and thatch the chancel: he shall lie above ground till he dance

a galliard about the churchyard, for Steeven
Loach.

WIG. *Sic argumentaris, Domine* Loach,—An we
make many such matches, we may pull down the
steeple, sell the bells and thatch the chancel ? In
good time, sir, and hang yourselves in the bell-ropes,
when you have done. *Domine, opponens præpono tibi
hanc quæstionem*, whether will you have the ground
broken or your pates broken first ? for one of them
shall be done presently, and to begin mine, I'll seal
it upon your coxcomb.

EUM. Hold thy hands, I pray thee, good fellow ;
be not too hasty.

COR. You capon's face, we shall have you turned
out of the parish one of these days, with never a
tatter to your back ; then you are in worse taking
than Jack.

EUM. Faith, and he is bad enough. This fellow
does but the part of a friend, to seek to bury his
friend : how much will bury him ?

WIG. Faith, about some fifteen or sixteen shillings
will bestow him honestly.

SEX. Ay, even thereabouts, sir.

EUM. Here, hold it, then :—[*aside*] and I have
left me but one poor three halfpence : now do I
remember the words the old man spake at the cross,
" Bestow all thou hast," and this is all, " till dead

men's bones come at thy call :"—here, hold it [*gives money*] ; and so farewell.

WIG. God, and all good, be with you, sir ! [*Exit* EUMENIDES]. Nay, you cormorants, I'll bestow one peal of Jack at mine own proper costs and charges.

COR. You may thank God the long staff and the bilbo-blade crossed not your coxcombs.—Well, we'll to the church-stile and have a pot, and so trill-lill.   [*Exit with* WIGGEN.

CHURCH. ⎱
            ⎰ Come, let's go.   [*Exeunt.*
SEX.   ⎰

FAN. But, hark you, gammer, methinks this Jack bore a great sway in the parish.

MADGE. O, this Jack was a marvellous fellow ! he was but a poor man, but very well beloved : you shall see anon what this Jack will come to.

Enter the HARVESTMEN *singing, with women in their hands.*

FRO. Soft ! who have we here ? our amorous harvesters.

FAN. Ay, ay, let us sit still, and let them alone.

Here the HARVESTMEN *sing, the song doubled.*

Lo, here we come a-reaping, a-reaping,
To reap our harvest-fruit!
And thus we pass the year so long,
And never be we mute.

[*Exeunt the* HARVESTMEN.

Enter HUANEBANGO.

FRO. Soft! who have we here?

MADGE. O, this is a choleric gentleman! All
you that love your lives, keep out of the smell of
his two-hand sword: now goes he to the conjurer.

FAN. Methinks the conjurer should put the fool
into a juggling-box.

HUAN. Fee, fa, fum,
        Here is the Englishman,—
        Conquer him that can,—
        Come for his lady bright,
        To prove himself a knight,
        And win her love in fight.

Enter COREBUS.

COR. Who-haw, Master Bango, are you here?

G 2

hear you, you had best sit down here, and beg an alms with me.

HUAN. Hence, base cullion! here is he that commandeth ingress and egress with his weapon, and will enter at his voluntary, whosoever saith no.

VOICE. No.

> [*A flame of fire; and* HUANEBANGO *falls down.*

MADGE. So with that they kissed, and spoiled the edge of as good a two-hand sword as ever God put life in. Now goes Corebus in, spite of the conjurer.

Enter SACRAPANT *and* TWO FURIES.

SAC. Away with him into the open fields,
To be a ravening prey to crows and kites:

> [HUAN. *is carried out by the* TWO FURIES.

And for this villain, let him wander up and down,
In naught but darkness and eternal night.

> [*Strikes* COREBUS *blind.*

. COR. Here hast thou slain Huan, a slashing
knight,
And robbéd poor Corebus of his sight.

SAC. Hence, villain, hence!   [*Exit* COREBUS.
                         Now I have unto Delia
Given a potion of forgetfulness,

That, when she comes, she shall not know her
    brothers.
Lo, where they labour, like to country-slaves,
With spade and mattock, on enchanted ground !
Now will I call her by another name ;
For never shall she know herself again
Until that Sacrapant hath breathed his last.
See where she comes.

Enter DELIA.

Come hither, Delia, take this goad ; here **hard**
At hand two slaves do work and dig for gold :
Gore them with this, and thou shalt have enough.
                          [Gives her a goad.
    DEL. Good sir, I know not what you mean.
    SAC. [*aside*]. She hath forgotten to be Delia,
But not forgot the name she should forget ;
But I will change her name.—
Fair Berecynthia, so this country calls you,
Go ply these strangers, wench ; they dig for gold.
                                [Exit.
    DEL. O heavens, how
Am I beholding to this fair young man !
But I must ply these strangers to their work :
See where they come.

Enter the Two Brothers *in their shirts, with spades,*
digging.

First Bro. O brother, see where Delia is !

Second Bro. O Delia,

Happy are we to see thee here !

Del. What tell you me of Delia, prating swains ?

I know no Delia, nor know I what you mean.

Ply you your work, or else you're like to smart.

    First Bro. Why, Delia, know'st . thou not thy
        brothers here ?

We come from Thessaly to seek thee forth ;

And thou deceiv'st thyself, for thou art Delia.

    Del. Yet more of Delia ? then take this, and
        smart :   [*Pricks them with the goad.*

What, feign you shifts for to defer your labour ?

Work, villains, work ; it is for gold you dig.

    Second Bro. Peace, brother, peace : this vile
        enchanter

Hath ravished Delia of her senses clean,

And she forgets that she is Delia.

    First Bro. Leave, cruel thou, to hurt the mise-
        rable.—

Dig, brother, dig, for she is hard as steel.

        [*Here they dig, and descry a light in a*
          glass under a little hill.

SECOND BRO. Stay, brother ; what hast thou
descried ?

DEL. Away, and touch it not ; 'tis something
that

My lord hath hidden there. [*Covers the light again.*

Re-enter SACRAPANT.

SAC. Well said ! thou plyest these pioners well.—
Go get you in, you labouring slaves.

[*Exeunt the* TWO BROTHERS.

Come, Berecynthia, let us in likewise,
And hear the nightingale record her notes. [*Exeunt.*

Enter ZANTIPPA, *to the Well of Life, with a pot in
her hand.*

ZAN. Now for a husband, house, and home : God
send a good one or none, I pray God ! My father
hath sent me to the well for the water of life, and
tells me, if I give fair words, I shall have a husband.
But here comes Celanta, my sweet sister : I'll stand
by and hear what she says. [*Retires.*

Enter CELANTA, *to the Well of Life, with a pot in
her hand.*

CEL. My father hath sent me to the well for

water, and he tells me, if I speak fair, I shall have a
husband, and none of the worst. Well, though I am
black, I am sure all the world will not forsake me ;
and, as the old proverb is, though I am black, I am
not the devil.

ZAN. [*coming forward*]. Marry-gup with a murren,
I know wherefore thou speakest that : but go thy
ways home as wise as thou camest, or I'll set thee
home with a wanion.

> [*Here she strikes her pitcher against her
> sister's, and breaks them both, and then
> exit.*

CEL. I think this be the curstest quean in the
world : you see what she is, a little fair, but as
proud as the devil, and the veriest vixen that lives
upon God's earth. Well, I'll let her alone, and go
home, and get another pitcher, and, for all this, get
me to the well for water.   [*Exit.*

Enter, out of SACRAPANT'S *cell, the* TWO FURIES,
carrying HUANEBANGO : *they lay him by the
Well of Life, and then exeunt. Re-enter* ZANTIPPA
with a pitcher to the well.

ZAN. Once again for a husband ; and, in faith,
Celanta, I have got the start of you ; belike husbands
grow by the well-side. Now my father says I must

rule my tongue : why, alas, what am I, then ? A woman without a tongue is as a soldier without his weapon : but I'll have my water, and be gone.

Here she offers to dip her pitcher in, and a HEAD *rises in the well.*

HEAD. Gently dip, but not too deep,
For fear you make the golden beard to weep,
Fair maiden, white and red,
Stroke me smooth, and comb my head,
And thou shalt have some cockell-bread.

ZAN. What is this ?
" Fair maiden, white and red,
    Comb me smooth, and stroke my head,
    And thou shalt have some cockell-bread ?"
" Cockell " callest thou it, boy ? faith, I'll give you cockell-bread.

She breaks her pitcher upon the HEAD : *then it thunders and lightens ; and* HUANEBANGO, *who is deaf and cannot hear, rises up.*

HUAN. Philida, phileridos, pamphilida, florida, flortos :
Dub dub-a-dub, bounce, quoth the guns, with a sul- phurous huff-snuff :
Waked with a wench, pretty peat, pretty iove and my sweet pretty pigsnie,

Just by thy side shall sit surnamed great Huanebango :
Safe in my arms will I keep thee, threat Mars, or
 thunder Olympus.

ZAN. [*aside*]. Foh, what greasy groom have we
here ? He looks as though he crept out of the
backside of the well, and speaks like a drum perished
at the west end.

HUAN. O, that I might,—but I may not, woe to
 my destiny therefore—
 Kiss that I clasp ! but I cannot : tell me, my destiny,
 wherefore ?

ZAN. [*aside*]. Whoop, now I have my dream.
Did you never hear so great a wonder as this, three
blue beans in a blue bladder, rattle, bladder, rattle ?

HUAN. [*aside*]. I'll now set my countenance, and
to her in prose ; it may be, this rim-ram-ruff is too
rude an encounter.—Let me, fair lady, if you be at
leisure, revel with your sweetness, and rail upon that
cowardly conjurer, that hath cast me, or congealed
me rather, into an unkind sleep, and polluted my
carcass.

ZAN. [*aside*]. Laugh, laugh, Zantippa ; thou hast
thy fortune, a fool and a husband under one.

HUAN. Truly, sweetheart, as I seem, about some
twenty years, the very April of mine age.

ZAN. [*aside*]. Why, what a prating ass is this !

HUAN. Her coral lips, her crimson chin,
Her silver teeth so white within,
Her golden locks, her rolling eye,
Her pretty parts, let them go by,
Heigh-ho, have wounded me,
That I must die this day to see!"

ZAN. . . . . thou art a flouting knave: "her coral
lips, her crimson chin!" ka,' wilshaw!

HUAN. True, my own, and my own because mine'
and mine because mine, ha, ha!—Above a thousand
pounds in possibility, and things fitting thy desire in
possession.

ZAN. [*aside*]. The sot thinks I ask of his lands.
Lob be your comfort. . . . . Hear you, sir; an if
you will have us, you had best say so betime.

HUAN. True, sweetheart, and will royalize thy
progeny with my pedigree.   [*Exeunt*

Enter EUMENIDES.

EUM. Wretched Eumenides, still unfortunate,
Envied by fortune and forlorn by fate,
Here pine and die, wretched Eumenides,
Die in the spring, the April of thy age!
Here sit thee down, repent what thou hast done:
I would to God that it were ne'er begun!

Enter the GHOST OF JACK.

G. OF JACK. You are well overtaken, sir.

EUM. Who's that?

G. OF JACK. You are heartily well met, sir.

EUM. Forbear, I say: who is that which pincheth me?

G. OF JACK. Trusting in God, good Master Eumenides, that you are in so good health as all your friends were at the making hereof,—God give you good morrow, sir! Lack you not a neat, handsome, and cleanly young lad, about the age of fifteen or sixteen years, that can run by your horse, and, for a need, make your mastership's shoes as black as ink? How say you, sir?

EUM. Alas, pretty lad, I know not how to keep myself, and much less a servant, my pretty boy; my state is so bad.

G. OF JACK. Content yourself, you shall not be so ill a master but I'll be as bad a servant. Tut, sir, I know you, though you know not me: are not you the man, sir, deny it if you can, sir, that came from a strange place in the land of Catita, where Jack-an-apes flies with his tail in his mouth, to seek out a lady as white as snow and as red as blood? Ha, ha! have I touched you now?

EUM. [*aside*]. I think this boy be a spirit.—How knowest thou all this ?

G. OF JACK. Tut, are not you the man, sir, deny it if you can, sir, that gave all the money you had to the burying of a poor man, and but one three half-pence left in your purse ? Content you, sir. I'll serve you, that is flat.

EUM. Well, my lad, since thou art so importunate, I am content to entertain thee, not as a servant, but a copartner in my journey. But whither shall we go? for I have not any money more than one bare three halfpence.

G. OF JACK. Well, master, content yourself; for if my divination be not out, that shall be spent at the next inn or alehouse we come to ; for, master, I know you are passing hungry: therefore I'll go before and provide dinner until that you come ; no doubt but you'll come fair and softly after.

EUM. Ay, go before ; I'll follow thee.

G. OF JACK. But do you hear, master ? do you know my name ?

EUM. No, I promise thee ; not yet.

G. OF JACK. Why, I am Jack.   [*Exit.*

EUM. Jack! why, be it so, then.

Enter the HOSTESS *and* JACK, *setting meat on the table; and Fiddlers come to play.* EUMENIDES *walks up and down, and will eat no meat.*

HOST. How say you, sir? do you please to sit down?

EUM. Hostess, I thank you, I have no great stomach.

HOST. Pray, sir, what is the reason your master is so strange? doth not this meat please him?

G. OF JACK. Yes, hostess, but it is my master's fashion to pay before he eats; therefore, a reckoning, good hostess.

HOST. Marry, shall you, sir, presently.　　*[Exit.*

EUM. Why, Jack, what dost thou mean? thou knowest I have not any money; therefore, sweet Jack, tell me what shall I do?

G. OF JACK. Well, master, look in your purse.

EUM. Why, faith, it is a folly, for I have no money.

G. OF JACK. Why, look you, master; do so much for me.

EUM. [*looking into his purse*]. Alas, Jack, my purse is full of money!

JACK. "Alas," master! does that word belong to this accident? why, methinks I should have seen you cast away your cloak, and in a bravado dance a galliard round about the chamber : why, master, your man can teach you more wit than this.

Re-enter HOSTESS.

Come, hostess, cheer up my master.

HOST. You are heartily welcome ; and if it please you to eat of a fat capon, a fairer bird, a finer bird, a sweeter bird, a crisper bird, a neater bird, your worship never eat of.

EUM. Thanks, my fine, eloquent hostess.

G. OF JACK. But hear you, master, one word by the way : are you content I shall be halves in all you get in your journey ?

EUM. I am, Jack ; here is my hand.

G. OF JACK. Enough, master, I ask no more.

EUM. Come, hostess, receive your money ; and I thank you for my good entertainment.

[*Gives money.*

HOST. You are heartily welcome, sir.

EUM. Come, Jack, whither go we now ?

G. OF JACK. Marry, master, to the conjurer's presently.

EUM. Content, Jack. — Hostess, farewell.

[*Exeunt.*

Enter COREBUS, *who is blind, and* CELANTA, *to the Well of Life for water.*

COR. Come, my duck, come: I have now got a wife: thou art fair, art thou not?

CEL. My Corebus, the fairest alive; make no doubt of that.

COR. Come, wench, are we almost at the well?

CEL. Ay, Corebus, we are almost at the well now. I'll go fetch some water: sit down while I dip my pitcher in.

A HEAD *comes up with ears of corn, which she combs into her lap.*

HEAD. Gently dip, but not too deep,
    For fear you make the golden beard to weep.
    Fair maiden, white and red,
    Comb me smooth, and stroke my head,
    And thou shalt have some cockell-bread.

A SECOND HEAD *comes up full of gold, which she combs into her lap.*

SEC. HEAD. Gently dip, but not too deep,
    For fear thou make the golden beard to weep.

Fair maid, white and red,

Comb me smooth, and stroke my head,

And every hair a sheaf shall be,

And every sheaf a golden tree.

CEL. O, see, Corebus, I have combed a great deal of gold into my lap, and a great deal of corn!

COR. Well said, wench! now we shall have just enough : God send us coiners to coin our gold. But come, shall we go home, sweetheart ?

CEL. Nay, come, Corebus, I will lead you.

COR. So, Corebus, things have well hit ;
Thou hast gotten wealth to mend thy wit. [*Exeunt.*

Enter the GHOST OF JACK *and* EUMENIDES.

G. OF JACK. Come away, master,, come.

EUM. Go along, Jack, I'll follow thee. Jack, they say it is good to go cross-legged, and say prayers backward ; how sayest thou ?

G. OF JACK. Tut, never fear, master ; let me alone. Here sit you still ; speak not a word ; and because you shall not be enticed with his enchanting speeches, with this same wool I'll stop your ears. [*Puts wool into the ears of* EUMENIDES.] And so, master, sit still, for I must to the conjurer. [*Exit.*

Enter SACRAPANT.

SAC. How now! what man art thou, that sits so
    sad?
Why dost thou gaze upon these stately trees
Without the leave and will of Sacrapant?
What, not a word but mum?   Then, Sacrapant,
Thou art betrayed.

Re-enter the GHOST OF JACK *invisible, and takes*
    SACRAPANT'S *wreath off from his head, and his*
    sword out of his hand.

What hand invades the head of Sacrapant?
What Fury doth envý my happy state?
Then, Sacrapant, these are thy latest days.
Alas, my veins are numbed, my sinews shrink,
My blood is pierced, my breath fleeting away,
And now my timeless date is come to end!
He in whose life his acts have been so foul,
Now in his death to hell descends his soul.   [*Dies.*

    G. OF JACK. O, sir, are you gone? now I hope
we shall have some other coil.—Now, master, how
like you this? the conjurer he is dead, and vows
never to trouble us more: now get you to your fair
lady, and see what you can do with her.—Alas, he

heareth me not all this while! but I will help that.

[*Pulls the wool out of the ears of* EU-MENIDES.

EUM. How now, Jack! what news?

G. OF JACK. Here, master, take this sword, and dig with it at the foot of this hill.　　[*Gives sword.*

[EUMENIDES *digs, and spies a light in a glass.*

EUM. How now, Jack! what is this?

G. OF JACK. Master, without this the conjurer could do nothing ; and so long as this light lasts, so long doth his art endure, and this being out, then doth his art decay.

EUM. Why then, Jack, I will soon put out this light.

G. OF JACK. Ay, master, how?

EUM. Why, with a stone I'll break the glass, and then blow it out.

G. OF JACK. No, master, you may as soon break the smith's anvil as this little vial ; nor the biggest blast that ever Boreas blew cannot blow out this little light ; but she that is neither maid, wife, nor widow. Master, wind this horn, and see what will happen.　　[*Gives horn.*

EUMENIDES *winds the horn.   Enter* VENELIA, *who
   breaks the glass, blows out the light, and then exit.*

So, master, how like you this? This is she that ran
madding in the woods, his betrothed love that
keeps the cross; and now, this light being out, all
are restored to their former liberty : and now, master,
to the lady that you have so long looked for.

The GHOST OF JACK *draws a curtain, and discovers*
   DELIA *sitting asleep.*

EUM. God speed, fair maid, sitting alone,—there
is once ; God speed, fair maid,—there is twice ; God
speed, fair maid,—that is thrice.

DEL. Not so, good sir, for you are by.

G. OF JACK. Enough, master, she hath spoke ;
now I will leave her with you.   [*Exit.*

EUM. Thou fairest flower of these western parts,
Whose beauty so reflecteth in my sight
As doth a crystal mirror in the sun ;
For thy sweet sake I have crossed the frozen
      Rhine ;
Leaving fair Po, I sailed up Danuby,
As far as Saba, whose enhancing streams
Cut twixt the Tartars and the Russians :

These have I crossed for thee, fair Delia :
Then grant me that which I have sued for long.

DEL. Thou gentle knight, whose fortune is so
good
To find me out and set my brothers free,
My faith, my heart, my hand I give to thee.

EUM. Thanks, gentle madam : but here comes
Jack ; thank him, for he is the best friend that we
have.

Re-enter the GHOST OF JACK, *with* SACRAPANT'S
head in his hand.

How now, Jack ! what hast thou there ?

G. OF JACK. Marry, master, the head of the
conjurer.

EUM. Why, Jack, that is impossible ; he was a
young man.

G. OF JACK. Ah, master, so he deceived them that
beheld him ! but he was a miserable, old, and
crooked man, though to each man's eye he seemed
young and fresh ; for, master, this conjurer took the
shape of the old man that kept the cross, and that
old man was in the likeness of the conjurer. But
now, master, wind your horn.

EUMENIDES *winds his horn.*   *Enter* VENELIA, *the*
        TWO BROTHERS, *and* ERESTUS.

EUM. Welcome, Erestus! welcome, fair Venelia!
Welcome, Thelea and Calypha both!
Now have I her that I so long have sought;
So saith fair Delia, if we have your consent.

FIRST BRO. Valiant Eumenides, thou well deserv'st
To have our favours; so let us rejoice
That by thy means we are at liberty:
Here may we joy each in the other's sight,
And this fair lady have her wandering knight.

G. OF JACK. So, master, now ye think you have
done; but I must have a saying to you: you know
you and I were partners, I to have half in all you
got.

EUM. Why, so thou shalt, Jack.

G. OF JACK. Why, then, master, draw your sword,
part your lady, let me have half of her presently.

EUM. Why, I hope, Jack, thou dost but jest: I
promised thee half I got, but not half my lady.

G. OF JACK. But what else, master? have you not
gotten her? therefore divide her straight, for I will
have half; there is no remedy.

EUM. Well, ere I will falsify my word unto my
friend, take her all: here, Jack, I'll give her thee.

G. OF JACK. Nay, neither more nor less, master, but even just half.

EUM. Before I will falsify my faith unto my friend, I will divide her : Jack, thou shalt have half.

FIRST BRO. Be not so cruel unto our sister, gentle knight.

SECOND BRO. O, spare fair Delia ! she deserves no death.

EUM. Content yourselves ; my word is passed to him.—Therefore prepare thyself, Delia, for thou must die.

DEL. Then farewell, world ! adieu, Eumenides !

      [EUMENIDES *offers to strike, and the* GHOST
         OF JACK *stays him.*

G. OF JACK. Stay, master ; it is sufficient I have tried your constancy. Do you now remember since you paid for the burying of a poor fellow ?

EUM. Ay, very well, Jack.

G. OF JACK. Then, master, thank that good deed for this good turn : and so God be with you all !

      [*Leaps down in the ground.*

EUM. Jack, what, art thou gone ? then farewell, Jack !—

Come, brothers, and my beauteous Delia,

Erestus, and thy dear Venelia,

We will to Thessaly with joyful hearts.

ALL. Agreed : we follow thee and Delia.

[*Exeunt all except* FROLIC, FANTASTIC, *and*
MADGE.

FAN. What, gammer, asleep ?

MADGE. By the mass, son, 'tis almost day ; and my windows shut at the cock's-crow.

FRO. Do you hear, gammer ? methinks this Jack bore a great sway amongst them.

MADGE. O, man, this was the ghost of the poor man that they kept such a coil to bury ; and that makes him to help the wandering knight so much. But come, let us in : we will have a cup of ale and a toast this morning, and so depart.

FAN. Then you have made an end of your tale, gammer ?

MADGE. Yes, faith : when this was done, I took a piece of bread and cheese, and came my way ; and so shall you have, too, before you go, to your breakfast.

[*Exeunt.*

POEMS.

POLYHYMNIA.

Written to celebrate the Completion of the 30th year of Elizabeth's reign 17th Nov. 1590

WHEREFORE, when thirty-two were come and
    gone,
Years of her reign, days of her country's peace,
Elizabeth, great empress of the world,
Britannia's Atlas, star of England's globe,
That sways the massy sceptre of her land,
And holds the royal reins of Albion ;
Began the gladsome sunny day to shine,
That draws in length date of her golden reign,
And thirty-three she numbereth in her throne,
That long in happiness and peace I pray
May number many to these thirty-three.
Wherefore it fares as whilom and of yore,
In armour bright and sheen fair England's
    knights,
In honour of their peerless sovereign,
High mistress of their service, thoughts, and
    lives,
Make to the tilt amain ; and trumpets sound,

And princely coursers neigh and champ the bit :
When all, addressed for deeds of high devoir,
Press to the sacred presence of their prince.

The First Couple.

SIR HENRY LEE. THE EARL OF CUMBERLAND.

Mighty in arms, mounted on puissant horse,
Knight of the crown, in rich embroidery,
And costly fair caparison charged with crowns,
O'ershadowed with a withered running vine,
As who would say, " My spring of youth is past,"
In corselet gilt of curious workmanship,
Sir Henry Lee, redoubted man-at-arms,
Leads in the troops : whom worthy Cumberland,
Thrice-noble earl, accoutred as became
So great a warrior and so good a knight,
Encountered first, y-clad in coat of steel,
And plumes and pendants all as white as swan,
And spear in rest, right ready to perform
What 'longed unto the honour of the place.
Together went these champions, horse and man,
Thundering along the tilt ; that at the shock
The hollow gyring vault of heaven resounds.
Six courses spent, and spears in shivers split,

The Second Couple.

THE LORD STRANGE. MASTER THOMAS GERRARD.

The Earl of Derby's valiant son and heir,
Brave Ferdinand Lord Strange, strangely em-
    barked
Under Jove's kingly bird the golden eagle,
Stanley's old crest and honourable badge,
As veering 'fore the wind in costly ship,
And armour white and watchet buckled fast,
Presents himself ; his horses and his men
Suited in satin to their master's colours,
Well near twice-twenty squires that went him by :
And having by his truchman pardon craved,
Vailing his eagle to his sovereign's eyes,
As who would say, " Stoop, eagle, to this sun,"
Dismounts him from his pageant, and attonce,
Taking his choice of lusty stirring horse
Covered with sumptuous rich caparisons,
He mounts him bravely for his friendly foe ;
And at the head he aims, and in his aim
Happily thrives, and breaks his azure staves.
Whom gentle Gerrard, all in white and green,
Colours belike best serving his conceit,
Lustily meets, mounted in seat of steel,
With flourishing plume and fair caparison ;

And then at every shock the shivers fly,
That recommend their honours to the sky.

The Third Couple.

THE LORD COMPTON.　MASTER HENRY NOWELL.

Next, in the virgin's colours, as before
Ran Cumberland, comes lovely Compton in ;
His courser trapped in white, and plumes and
　　staves
Of snowy hue, and squires in fair array,
Waiting their lord's good fortune in the field ;
His armour glittering like the moon's bright rays,
Or that clear silver path, the milk-white way,
That in Olympus leads to Jove's high court.
Him noble-minded Nowell pricks to meet,
All armed in sables, with rich bandalier,
That baldrick-wise he ware, set with fair stones
And pearls of Inde, that like a silver bend
Showed on his varnished corselet black as jet;
And beauteous plumes and bases suitable ;
And on his stirrup waits a trusty train
Of servants clad in purple liveries :
And to't they go, this lord and lusty knight,
To do their royal mistress honour's right.

The Fourth Couple.

THE LORD BURKE. SIR EDWARD DENNY.

When, mounted on his fierce and foaming
    steed,
In riches and in colours like his peers,
With ivory plumes, in silver-shining arms,
His men in crimson dight and staves in red,
Comes in Lord Burke, a fair young Ireland
    lord,
Bent chiefly to the exercise of arms ;
And bounding in his princely mistress' eye,
Chargeth his staff, when trumpet calls away,
At noble Denny's head, brave man-at-arms,
That furiously, with flaming sword in hand,
(As if the God of War had sent him down,
Or, if you will, to show his burning zeal
And forwardness in service of her person,
To whom those martial deeds were conse-
    crate,)
Speeds to the tilt amain, rich as the rest ;
Himself, his horse, his pages, all in green,
Green velvet, fairly garnished horse and
    man.

The Fifth Couple.

THE EARL OF ESSEX.   MASTER FULKE GREVILLE.

Then proudly shocks amid the martial throng
Of lusty lanciers, all in sable sad,
Drawn on with coal-black steeds of dusky hue,
In stately chariot full of deep device,
Where gloomy Time sat whipping on the team,
Just back to back with this great champion,—
Young Essex, that thrice-honourable earl ;
Y-clad in mighty arms of mourner's dye,
And plume as black as is the raven's wing,
That from his armour borrowed such a light
As boughs of yew receive from shady stream :
His staves were such, or of such hue at least,
As are those banner-staves that mourners bear ;
And all his company in funeral black ;
As if he mourned to think of him he missed,
Sweet Sidney, fairest shepherd of our green,
Well-lettered warrior, whose successor he
In love and arms had ever vowed to be :
In love and arms, O, may he so succeed
As his deserts, as his desires would speed !
With this great lord must gallant Greville run,
Fair man-at-arms, the Muses' favourite,
Lover of learning and of chivalry,

Sage in his saws, sound judge of poesy ;
That lightly mounted makes to him amain,
In armour gilt and bases full of cost.
Together go these friends as enemies ;
As when a lion in a thicket pent,
Spying the boar all bent to combat him,
Makes through the shrubs and thunders as he
goes.

The Sixth Couple.

SIR CHARLES BLOUNT. MASTER THOMAS VAVASOUR.

And then, as blithe as bird of morning's light,
Inflamed with honour, glistering as the sun
What time he mounts the sweating lion's back,
Beset with glorious sunshine of his train,
Bearing the sun upon his arméd breast,
That like a precious shining carbuncle,
Or Phœbus' eye, in heaven itself reflects,—
Comes Sir Charles Blount, in or and azure
dight ;
Rich in his colours, richer in his thoughts,
Rich in his fortune, honour, arms, and art.
And him the valiant Vavasour assails,
On fierce and ready horse, with spear in rest,
In orange-tawny, bright and beautiful,
Himself, his men, and all: and on they speed,

II

And haste they make to meet, and meet they do,
And do the thing for which they meet in haste ;
Each in his armour amiable to see,
That in their looks bear love and chivalry.

The Seventh Couple.

MASTER ROBERT CAREY.   MASTER WILLIAM GRESHAM.

By this the trump called Carey to the tilt,
Fair bird, fair cygnet of our silver swan ;
When, like a lord in pomp and princely show,
And like a champion fitted for the war,
And not unlike the son of such a sire,
Under a plume of murrey and of white
That like a palm-tree beautifully spread,
On mighty horse of Naples mounted fair,
And horse at hand and men and pages pight,
All with a Burning Heart greets he her grace,
Whose gracious countenance he his heaven esteems,
And to her sacred person it presents,
As who would say, "My heart and life is hers,
To whom my loyalty this heart prefers."
And at the summons out his foeman flies,
Gresham, the heir of golden Gresham's land,
That beautified New Troy with Royal Change,
Badge of his honour and magnificence ;

Silver and sable, such his colours were,
And ready was his horse, and readier he,
To bound, and well behave him in her eye,
Upon whose looks his life and honour stood.
Then horse and man conspired to meet amain ;
Along the tilt Carey and Gresham go,
Swift as the swallow, or that Greekish nymph
That seemed to overfly the ears of corn :
And break they do, they miss not, as I ween,
And all was done in honour of their queen.

The Eighth Couple.

Sir William Knowles.   Master Anthony Cooke.

Then, like the three Horatii in the field,
Betwixt the Roman and the Alban camp,
That triumphed in the royal right of Rome,
Or old Duke Aymon's glory, Dordogne's pride,
Came in the noble English Nestor's sons,
Brave Knowles his offspring, hardy champions ;
Each in his plumes, his colours, and device,
Expressing warrior's wit and courtier's grace.
    Against Sir William ran a lusty knight ;
Fine in device he was and full of wit,
Famous beyond the chalky British cliffs,
And loved and honoured in his country's bounds,

H 2

Anthony Cooke, a man of noble mind,
For arms and courtship equal to the best :
Valour and Virtue sat upon his helm,
Whom Love and lowering Fortune led along,
And Life and Death he portrayed in his show ;
A liberal Hand, badge of nobility,
A Heart that in his mistress' honour vows
To task his hand in witness of his heart,
Till age shake off war's rough habiliments.
Then with such cunning can they couch their
    staves,
That worthily each knight himself behaves.

The Ninth Couple.

SIR THOMAS KNOWLES.   SIR PHILIP BUTLER.

The youngest brother, Mars his sworn man,
That won his knightly spurs in Belgia,
And followed dub of drum in fortune's grace,
Well horsed and armed, Sir Philip Butler greets ;
The noble Essex' friend and follower,
In mourning sable dight by sympathy,
A gentle knight ; and meekly at the tilt
He stands, as one that had no heart to hurt
His friendly foe : but at the trumpet's sound
He flies along ; and bravely at the face

His force he bends : the rival of his fame
Spurs on his steed, nor shuns the shock for fear ;
And so they meet ; the armour bears the scar
Of this encounter and delightful war.

The Tenth Couple.

MASTER ROBERT KNOWLES.   MASTER RALPH BOWES.

The last, not least, of these brave brethren,
Laden with honour and with golden boughs,
Entering the lists, like Titan armed with fire
When in the queachy plot Python he slew,
Bowes takes to task with strong and mighty arm,
Right richly mounted : horse and man it seemed
Were well agreed to serve as roughly there
As in the enemy's reach for life they would ;
And, when they ran, methought a tempest rose,
That in the storm the clattering armours sound,
As horse and man had both been borne to ground.

The Eleventh Couple.

MASTER THOMAS SIDNEY.   MASTER ROBERT ALEXANDER.

Thus long hath dainty Sidney sat and seen
Honour and Fortune hover in the air,

That from the glorious beams of England's
    eye
Came streaming; Sidney, at which name I
    sigh,
Because I lack the Sidney that I loved,
And yet I love the Sidneys that survive.
    Thus long, I say, sat Sidney and beheld
The shivers fly of many a shaken spear;
When, mounted on a courser trapped in white,
And throughly well-appointed he and his,
Pure sparks of virtue kindling honour's fire,
He thought he might, and, for he might, he
    would
Reach at this glory,—fair befall him still!—
And to the tilt, impatient of delay,
He comes, encountered with a threatening point
That Alexander menaced to him fast,
A valorous and lusty gentleman,
Well-fitted with his armour and his steed;
And him young Sidney sits, and had he charged
The Macedonian Alexander's staff,
He had been answered by that valiant youth:
So well behaved himself this fair young knight,
As Paris had to great Achilles' lance
Applied his tender fingers and his force.

The Twelfth Couple.

MASTER JOHN NEDHAM.   MASTER RICHARD ACTON.

The next came Nedham in on lusty horse,
That, angry with delay, at trumpet's sound
Would snort, and stamp, and stand upon no
    ground,
Unwilling of his master's tarriance :
Yet tarry must his master, and with him
His prancing steed ; till trumpets sounding shrill
Made Acton spur apace, that, with applause
Of all beholders, hied him lustily,
As who would say, "Now go I to the goal :"
And then they ride, and run, and take their
    chance,
As death were fixed at point of either's lance.

The Thirteenth Couple.

MASTER CHARLES DAVERS.   MASTER EVERARD DIGBY.

Now drew this martial exercise to end ;
And Davers here and Digby were the last
Of six-and-twenty gallant gentlemen,
Of noble birth and princely resolution,
That ran in compliment, as you have heard,

In honour of their mistress' holiday;
A gracious sport, fitting that golden time,
The day, the birthday of our happiness,
The blooming time, the spring of England's
   peace.
Peace, then, my Muse; yet, ere thou peace
   report,
Say how thou saw'st these actors play their
   parts,
Both mounted bravely, bravely minded both,
Second to few or none for their success;
Their high devoir, their deeds do say no less.

   And now had England's queen, fair England's
      life,
Beheld her lords, and lovely lordly knights,
Do honour's service to their sovereign:
And heaven by this distilled down tears of joy,
In memory and honour of this day.

SIR HENRY LEE *resigns his place of honour at tilt to*
   the EARL OF CUMBERLAND.

And now, as first by him intended was,
In sight of prince, and peers, and people round,
Old Henry Lee, Knight of the Crown, dismounts;
And in a fair pavilion hard at hand,

Where holy lights burned on the hallowed shrine
To Virtue or to Vesta consecrate,
Having unarmed his body, head and all,
To his great mistress his petition makes ;
That, in regard and favour of his age,
It would so please her princely majesty
To suffer him give up his staff and arms,
And honourable place wherein he served,
To that thrice-valiant earl whose honour's pledge
His life should be.   With that he singled forth
The flower of English knights, the valiant Earl
Of Cumberland ; and him, before them all,
He humbly prays her highness to accept,
And him instal in place of those designs ;
And to him gives his armour and his lance,
Protesting to her princely majesty,
In sight of heaven and all her lovely lords,
He would betake him to his orisons,
And spend the remnant of his waning age,
Unfit for wars and martial exploits,
In prayers for her endless happiness.
Whereat she smiles, and sighs, and seemed to say,
" Good woodman, though thy green be turned to
        grey,
Thy age past April's prime and pleasant May,
Have thy request ; we take him at thy praise :
May he succeed the honour of thy days !"

" Amen," said all, and hope they do no less ;
No less his virtue and nobility,
His skill in arms and practice promiseth.
And many champions such may England live to
　　have,
And days and years as many such as she in heart
　　can crave !

ANGLORUM FERIÆ.

written to Celebrate the Completion of the 37 year of Elizabeth's reign 17th Novr. 1595.

DESCEND, ye sacred daughters of King Jove:
Apollo, spread thy sparkling wings to mount,
And try some lightsome sweet Castalian springs
That warble to their silver-winding waves,
Making soft music in their gentle glide:
Clio, the sagest of these Sisters Nine,
Conduct thy learnèd company to court,
Eliza's court, Astræa's earthly heaven;
There take survey of England's empress,
And in her praise tune your heroic songs:
Write, write, you chroniclers of time and fame
That keep Remembrance' golden register,
And recommend to time's eternity
Her honour's height and wonders of her age,
Wonders of her that reason's reach transcend,
Such wonders as have set the world at gaze;
Write, write, you chroniclers of time and fame,
Elizabeth by miracles preserved
From perils imminent and infinite:

Clio, proclaim with golden trump and pen
Her happy days, England's high holidays ;
O'er Europe's bounds take wing, and make thy
    flight
Through melting air, from where the rising sun
Gallops the zodiac in his fiery wain,
Even to the brink where Thetis in her bower
Of pumey and tralucent pebble-stones
Receives the weary bridegroom of the sea ;
Beyond Grand Cair, by Nilus' slimy bank,
Over the wild and sandy Afric plains ;
Along the frozen shore of Tanais,
Whose icy crust Apollo cannot thaw ;
Even there and round about this earthly ball
Proclaim the day of England's happiness,
The days of peace, the days of quietness,
And let her gladsome birthday be the first,
Her day of birth, beginning of our bliss ;
Set down the day in characters of gold,
And mark it with a stone as white as milk,
That cheerful sunny day.   Wear eglantine,
And wreaths of roses red and white put on
In honour of that day, you lovely nymphs,
And pæans sing and sweet melodious songs ;
Along the chalky cliffs of Albion
Lead England's lovely shepherds in a dance
O'er hill and dale, and downs, and daisy-plots,

And be that day England's high holiday ;
And holidays and high days be they all,
High holidays, days, minutes, months, and hours,
That multiply the number of her years ;
Years that for us beget this golden age,
Wherein we live in safety under her,
Wherein she reigns in honour over us :
So may she long and ever may she so,
Untouched of traitorous hand or treacherous foe!

    Her birthday being celebrated thus,
Clio, record how she hath been preserved,
Even in the gates of death and from her youth,
To govern England in the ways of truth ;
Record heaven's goodness to this gracious queen,
Whose virtue's peer what age hath ever seen ?

    To pass the story of her younger days,
And stormy tempest happily o'erblown,
Wherein by mercy and by miracle
She was rescúed for England's happiness,
And comfort of the long-afflicted flock
That strayed like scattered sheep scared from the
     fold ;
To slip remembrance of those careful days,
Days full of danger, happy days withal,
Days of her preservation and defence ;
Behold the happiest day, the holiday
That young and old and all do celebrate,

The day of joy, the day of jollity!
The best of all the days that we have seen
Was wherein she was crownéd England's Queen,
Elizabeth, anointed of the Highest
To sit upon her kingly father's seat,
And wear in honour England's diadem,
To sway that massy sceptre and that sword
That awed the world in his triumphant hand,
And now in her's commands the enemy,
And with dishonour drives the daring foe
Back to his den, tired with successless arms,
Wearied with wars by land and wreck by sea.
Muses and Graces, gods and goddesses,
Adorn, adore, and celebrate this day.
The meanest with the mightiest may in this
Express his love ; for loyalty alike
Blazons affection's force in lord and lown.

    In honour of this happy day, behold
How high and low, the young and old in years,
England, hath put a face of gladness on,
And court and country carol in her praise,
And in her honour tune a thousand lays!
    With just return of this triumphant day,
And prosperous revolution of the same,
Auspiciously beginning many years
And golden days and infinite to come,
Passing in number and in happiness

The best that ever earthly prince enjoyed
By sufferance of the highest King of kings ;
Behold, in honour of this holiday,
What pæans loud triumphant London sings,
What holy tunes and sacrifice of thanks
England's metropolis as incense sends !
And in the sound of cymbals, trumps, and shalms,
In honour of his noble mistress' name,
To whom his life he owes and offers up,
Lo, London's shepherd, guardian of his flock,
Praiseth the Mighty One of Israel,
And with the strings of his unfeignéd heart
Tunes his true joy for all those days of peace,
Those quiet days that Englishmen enjoy
Under our queen, fair queen of Brut's New
    Troy !
   With whom in sympathy and sweet accord
All loyal subjects join, and hearts and hands
Lift up to Heaven's high throne, and sacrifice
Of praises and of hearty prayers send
Thanksgiving for our blessings and the grace,
The gracious blessings on that day poured down
On England's head ; that day whereon this queen
Inaugured was and holily installed,
Anointed of the highest King of kings,
In her hereditary royal right
Successively to sit enthronizéd.

And in this general plaudit and applause,
And celebration of this joyful day,
Wherein pale Envy, vanquished long ago,
Gave way to Virtue's great deserts in her,
And wounded with remembrance of her name
Made hence amain to murmur that abroad
He durst not openly disgorge at home,
In his own nest filled with so foul a bird,
And breathe his discontentments over sea
Among those erring fugitives that pine
At England's prosperous peace, and nothing
    more
Do thirst than alteration of the state,
And nothing less than our good queen affect ;
A number of unnatural Englishmen,
That curse the day so happy held of us,
Whose base revolt from their allegiance due
To prince and country makes them infamous,
Condemned among the Turks and Infidels,
False architects of those foul practices
That end in their dishonour and their shame,
Those bloody stratagems, those traitorous trains,
And cruel siege they lay unto her life,
Precious in sight of heaven and dear to us,
Her loving and her loyal subjects all,
Whom Jacob's God hath many ways preserved,
Yea, even betwixt the bridge and water's brink,

Saving her as by miracle in the fall
From Pharaoh's rod and from the sword of
    Saul :—
Lo, in this triumph that true subjects make,
Envied of none but enemies of the truth,
Her enemies, that serves the living Lord
And puts in him her confidence and trust,
Thou, sacred Muse of History, describe,
That all may see how well she is beloved,
What troop of loyal English knights in arms,
Right richly mounted and appointed all,
In shining arms accoutred for the war,
Small number of a number numberless,
Held justs in honour of her holiday,
Ready to do their duties and devoir
Against the mightiest enemy she hath,
Under what clime soe'er his colours wave,
And with keen sword and battle-axe in hand
To wound his crest, whatever foe he be
That any way in her dishonour braves.
    Among this stirring company of knights,
That at the tilt in fair habiliments
Gan show themselves, renownéd Cumberland,
Knight of the Crown, in gilded armour dight,
Mounted at Queen Elizabeth's approach,
Inflamed with honour's fire, and left his hold
Kept by a dragon, laden with fair spoils :

And there his duty done, and large device
Made by his page known to her Majesty,
Whose gracious eye reflecting on this earl
Was like Prometheus' life-infusing fire,
Behold, he stands impatient of delay,
Awaiting there his friendly foe's approach !
Daring he stands, true knight and challenger,
And hardly brooks the time of their address
That shortly came in duty all devote,
To solace with their martial exercise
Their princely mistress, to whose worthiness
That day's device and days of all their lives
Right humbly were and purely dedicate.

  The first that led, in cheerful colours clad,
In innocent white and fair carnation,
Was he whose wisdom in his younger years
And love to arms make him so far renowned,
The noble Earl of Essex and of Ewe.
His mute approach and action of his mutes
Said that he was solicited diversely ;
One way to follow war and war's designs,—
And well he may, for skill he can full well
Of war's adventures, 'larms, and stratagems ;—
Another way t' apply him to the care
Of commonweal affairs, and show the way
To help to underbear with grave advice
The weighty beam whereon the state depends:

Well may he this way or the other take,
And both shall his nobility become ;
The gravity and greatness of the one
Shall beautify the other's worthiness ;
His senate-robes shall beautify his arms,
His chivalry nobilitate his name.

Then Sussex, seated on his champing steed,
Dreadful to see, and in sad tawny dight,
Came in, as if some angry man of war
Had charged his lance and put himself in arms,
Under an eben-tree or blasted yew :
Such showed his plume, or like in my conceit
To ravens' feathers by the moon's reflex,
Shining where night by day doth take repose.
Mars in his wrath sitting upon his drum,
Devising tragedies, strikes no greater fear
Into the eyes and hearts of earthly men,
Than did methought this champion in his way ;
Nor in his doings ever man-at-arms
So young of years more forward than this earl :
So prone, so puissant, and successful still
In all his courses was this warlike knight.

Then Bedford and Southampton made up
    five,
Five valiant English earls. Southampton ran
As Bevis of Southampton, that good knight,
Had justed in the honour of the day ;

And certes Bevis was a mighty man,
Valiant in arms, gentle and debonair,
And such was young Wriothesley, that came
As if in duty to his sovereign
And honour's race for all that he had done,
He would be of the noblest overrun.
Like to himself and to his ancestors,
Ran Bedford, to express his readiness,
His love to arms, his loyalty to her
Whose burning eyeballs did retain the heat
That kindled honour's fire at their hearts ;
Bravely ran Bedford, and his staves he brake
Right happily for his high mistress' sake.

   Compton of Compton came in shining arms,
Well mounted and appointed for the field,
A gallant lord ; richly arrayed was he,
He and his train.   Clio, recount his fame ;
Record with me his love to learning's lore,
And valiant doings on this holiday :
Short will I be in process of his praise ;
Courageously he ran, and with the best
From forth the field bare honour on his crest.

   Carew was well-acquainted with the place,
And to the tilt proudly he made approach ;
His steed well-taught, himself fitted in all,
Fell to his noble exercise of arms,
And on his courser gan himself advance,

Whose neighs and plays were princely to behold :
Remembrance of this day revived this knight ;
His turn he takes, and at the trumpet's sound
Breaks at the head with many a lofty bound.

    In bases and caparisons of cost
Came three redoubted knights and men-at-arms,
Old Knowles his offspring, gallant cavaliers ;
And such they showed as were King Arthur's
    knights
He whilom used to feast at Camelot,
Or three of great King Priam's valiant sons
Had left Elysium and the fields of Mars
To celebrate Eliza's holiday :
They ran as if three Hectors had made way
To meet Achilles, Ajax, Diomede.
Palm had the eldest branching of his crest :
'Tis hard to say which brother did the best.

    Like Venus' son in Mars his armour clad,
Beset with glorious globes and golden flames,
Came Dudley in ; nor shall it me become
To dive into the depth of his device ;
Rich in his thoughts and valiant in his deeds,
No whit dishonoured by his fainting horse,
That cowardlike would have held his master
    back
From honour's goal,—ill-natured and ill-taught,
To fail him foully in so great a presence.

But as an archer with a bended bow
The farther from the mark he draws his shaft,
The farther flies it and with greater force
Wounds earth and air ; so did it fare in this :
This lusty runner, thus restrained at first,
Now all inflamed, soon having changed his
        steed,
And viewed the person of his princely mistress,
Whose radiant beams have power to set on fire
The icy ridge of snowy Rhodope,
Flies like a bullet from a cannon's mouth.
His arméd horse made dreadful harmony,
Grating against the rails : so valiantly
He justed, that unjust it were in me
Not to admire young Dudley's chivalry.

Young Howard, ramping lion-like, came on,
Anchor of Howard's honourable house,
His noble father's hope, his mother's joy.
Loyal and lovely was this fair young knight,
Gracious in his beginnings at the tilt,
Pleasing to her to whom he did present
His person and the service of that day,
And all the days and minutes of his life :
Bravely he bare him in his mistress' eye,
And brake his staves and let the shivers fly.

Drury in flames of gold embroidered fair,
Inflamed with love of virtue and of arms,

Came to the tilt like Phœbus,
And like a warrior there demeaned himself;
Heaven's vault, earth's centre sounded of his
 force:
So well he ran as they that do him right,
For field and court held him a worthy knight.

 Among these runners that in virtue's race
Contended, rivals of each other's praise,
Nowell and Needham, gentlemen of name,
Came mounted and appointed gallantly;
Both nobly minded, as became them well,
Resolved to run in honour of the day.

 L'éscu d'amour, the arms of loyalty,
Lodged Skydmore in his heart; and on he
 came,
And well and worthily demeaned himself
In that day's service: short and plain to be,
Nor lord nor knight more forward than was he.

 Then Ratcliffe, Reynolds, Blount, and Carey
 came,
In all accoutrements fitting gentlemen;
Well mounted and appointed every man;
And gallantly and worthily they ran.

 Long may they run in honour of the day!
Long may she live to do them honour's right,
To grace their sports and them as she hath
 done,

England's Astræa, Albion's shining sun!
And may she shine in beauty fresh and sheen
Hundreds of years, our thrice-renownéd queen!
Write, Clio, write; write, and record her story,
Dear in Heaven's eye, her court and country's
    glory.

A FAREWELL (1589)

INTITULED

TO THE FAMOUS AND FORTUNATE GENERALS OF OUR ENGLISH FORCES BY LAND AND SEA, SIR JOHN NORRIS AND SIR FRANCIS DRAKE, KNIGHTS.

HAVE done with care, my hearts! aboard amain,
With stretching sails to plough the swelling waves :
Bid England's shore and Albion's chalky cliffs
Farewell ; bid stately Troynovant adieu,
Where pleasant Thames from Isis' silver head
Begins her quiet glide, and runs along
To that brave bridge, the bar that thwarts her
    course,
Near neighbour to the ancient stony Tower,
The glorious hold that Julius Cæsar built.
Change love for arms ; girt-to your blades, my
    boys !
Your rests and muskets take, take helm and targe,
And let God Mars his consort make you mirth,—
The roaring cannon, and the brazen trump,

The angry-sounding drum, the whistling fife,
The shrieks of men, the princely courser's neigh.
Now vail your bonnets to your friends at home :
Bid all the lovely British dames adieu,
That under many a standard well-advanced
Have hid the sweet alarms and braves of love ;
Bid theatres and proud tragedians,
Bid Mahomet, Scipio, and mighty Tamburlaine,
King Charlemagne, Tom Stukeley, and the rest,
Adieu.   To arms, to arms, to glorious arms !
With noble Norris, and victorious Drake,
Under the sanguine cross, brave England's badge,
To propagate religious piety,
And hew a passage with your conquering swords
By land and sea, wherever Phœbus' eye,
Th' eternal lamp of heaven, lends us light ;
By golden Tagus, or the western Inde,
Or through the spacious bay of Portugal,
The wealthy ocean-main, the Tyrrhene sea,
From great Alcides' pillars branching forth
Even to the gulf that leads to lofty Rome :
There to deface the pride of Antichrist,
And pull his paper walls and popery down,—
A famous enterprise for England's strength ;
To steel your swords on Avarice' triple crown,
And cleanse Augeas' stalls in Italy.
To arms, my fellow-soldiers ! Sea and land

Lie open to the voyage you intend ;
And sea or land, bold Britons, far or near,
Whatever course your matchless virtue shapes,
Whether to Europe's bounds, or Asian plains,
To Afric's shore, or rich America,
Down to the shades of deep Avernus' crags,
Sail on, pursue your honours to your graves :
Heaven is a sacred covering for your heads,
And every climate virtue's tabernacle.
To arms, to arms, to honourable arms !
Hoise sails, weigh anchors up, plough up the seas
With flying keels, plough up the land with swords :
In God's name venture on ; and let me say
To you, my mates, as Cæsar said to his,
Striving with Neptune's hills ; "You bear," quoth
     he,
"Cæsar and Cæsar's fortune in your ships."
You follow them, whose swords successful are :
You follow Drake, by sea the scourge of Spain,
The dreadful dragon, terror to your foes,
Victorious in his return from Inde,
In all his high attempts unvanquishéd.
You follow noble Norris, whose renown,
Won in the fertile fields of Belgia,
Spreads by the gates of Europe to the courts
Of Christian kings and heathen potentates.
You fight for Christ, and England's peerless queen

Elizabeth, the wonder of the world,
Over whose throne the enemies of God
Have thundered erst their vain successless braves.
O, ten-times-treble happy men, that fight
Under the cross of Christ and England's queen,
And follow such as Drake and Norris are!
All honours do this cause accompany ;
All glory on these endless honours waits :
These honours and this glory shall He send,
Whose honour and whose glory you defend.

Yours, G. P.

THE RIGHT HON. EARL OF ESSEX

HIS WELCOME INTO ENGLAND FROM PORTUGAL.

A.D. 1589.

PIERS.

DICITE, Iö pæan, et, Iö, bis dicite, pæan !
In patriam rediit magnus Apollo suam.

PALINODE.

Herdgroom, what gars thy pipe to go so loud ?
Why bin thy looks so smicker and so proud ?
Perdy, plain Piers, but this couth ill agree
With thilk bad fortune that aye thwarteth thee.

PIERS.

That thwarteth me, good Palinode, is fate,
Y-born was Piers to be infortunate ;
Yet shall my bagpipe go so loud and shrill
That heaven may entertain my kind goodwill ;

Iö, iö pæan !

PALINODE.

Sot, I say, losel, lewdest of all swains,
Sing'st thou proud pæans on these open plains?
So ill sitteth this strain, this lofty note,
With thy rude tire and grey russet coat.

PIERS.

Grey as my coat is, green all are my cares,
My grass to dross, my corn is turned to tares;
Yet even and morrow will I never lin
To make my crowd speak as it did begin;

        Iö, iö pæan!

PALINODE.

Thou art too crank, and crowdest all too high;
Beware a chip fall not into thine eye:
Man, if triumphals here be in request,
Then let them chant them that can chant them best.

PIERS.

Thou art a sour swain, Palinode, perdy;
My bagpipe vaunteth not of victory:
Then give my leave sonizance to make
For chivalry and lovely learning's sake;

        Iö, iö pæan!

PALINODE.

Thou hardy herdsman, dar'st thou of arms chant ?
Sike verse, I tell thee, ought have a great vaunt :
Then how may thy boldness scape a fine frump ?
War's laud is matter for the brazen trump.

PIERS.

Of arms to sing I have nor lust nor skill ;
Enough is me to blazon my goodwill,
To welcome home, that long hath lackéd been,
One of the jolliest shepherds of our green ;

Iö, iö pæan !

PALINODE.

Tell me, good Piers, I pray thee tell it me
What may thilk jolly swain or shepherd be,
Or whence y-comen, that he thus welcome is,
That thou art all so blithe to see his bliss ?

PIERS.

Palinode, thou makest a double demand,
Which I will answer as I understand ;
Yet will I not forget, so God me mend,
To pipe loud pæans as my stanzas end ;

Iö, iö pæan !

Thilk shepherd, Palinode, whom my pipe praiseth,
Whose glory my reed to the welkin raiseth,
He's a great herdgroom, certes, but no swain,
Save hers that is the flower of Phœbe's plain ;

Iö, iö pæan !

He's well allied and lovéd of the best,
Well-thewed, fair and frank, and famous by his
    crest ;
His Rein-deer, racking with proud and stately
    pace,
Giveth to his flock a right beautiful grace ;

Iö, iö pæan !

He waits where our great shepherdess doth wun,
He playeth in the shade, and thriveth in the sun ;
He shineth on the plains, his lusty flock him by,
As when Apollo kept in Arcady ;

Iö, iö pæan !

Fellow in arms he was in their flow'ring days
With that great shepherd, good Philisides ;
And in sad sable did I see him dight,
Moaning the miss of Pallas' peerless knight ;

Iö, iö pæan !

With him he served, and watched, and waited late,
To keep the grim wolf from Eliza's gate ;

And for their mistress, thoughten these two swains,
They moughten never take too mickle pains ;

> Iö, iö pæan !

But, ah for grief! that jolly groom is dead,
For whom the Muses silver tears have shed ;
Yet in this lovely swain, source of our glee,
Mun all his virtues sweet reviven be ;

> Iö, iö pæan !

PALINODE.

So moughten they, Piers, and happily thrive
To keepen this herdsman after death alive :
But whence, I pray thee tell me, come is he,
For whom thy pipe and pæans make such glee ?

PIERS.

Certes, Sir Shepherd, comen he is from far.
From wrath of deepest seas and storm of war,
Safe is he come—O swell, my pipe, with joy !—
To the old buildings of new-rearéd Troy ;

> Iö, iö pæan !

Fron sea, from shore, where he with swink and
sweat
Felt foeman's rage and summer's parching heat,

I

Safe is he come, laden with honour's spoil :
O swell, my pipe, with joy, and break the while ;

> Iö, iö pæan !

PALINODE.

Thou foolish swain that thus art overjoyed,
How soon may here thy courage be accoyed !
If he be one come new from western coast,
Small cause hath he, or thou for him, to boast.

I see no palm, I see no laurel-boughs
Circle his temples or adorn his brows ;
I hear no triumphs for this late return,
But many a herdsman more disposed to mourn.

PIERS.

Pale lookest thou, like spite, proud Palinode ;
Venture doth loss, and war doth danger bode :
But thou art of those harvesters, I see,
Would at one shock spoil all the filberd-tree ;

> Iö, iö pæan !

For shame, I say, give virtue honours due !
I'll please the shepherd but by telling true :
Palm mayst thou see and bays about his head,
That all his flock right forwardly hath led :

> Iö, iö pæan !

But, woe is me, lewd lad, fame's full of lies,
Envy doth aye true honour's deeds despise ;
Yet chivalry will mount with glorious wings,
Spite all, and nestle near the seat of kings ;

Iö, iö pæan !

Base thrall is he that is foul slander's slave :
To pleasen all what wight may him behave ?
Yea, Jove's great son, though he were now alive,
Mought find no way thilk labour to achive ;

Iö, iö pæan !

ALINODE.

Well plead'st thou, gentle lad, for this great peer :
Then tell me, sith but thou and I am here,
Did not thilk bagpipe, man, which thou dost blow,
A Farewell on our soldiers erst bestow ?

How is't, then, thilk great shepherd of the field,
To whom our swains sike humble 'beisance yield,
And thou these lauds and labours seriously,
Was in that work not mentioned specially ?

PIERS.

Hark, Palinode, me dare not speak too loud ;
Hence was he raught, wrapt in a fiery cloud,

I 2

With Mars his viceroy and a golden drake,
So that of him me durst no notice take ;

Iö, iö pæan !

But now returned, to royalize his fame,
Whose mighty thoughts at honours trophies aim,
Lest worthily I moughten witned be,
I welcome him with shepherd's country glee ;

Iö, iö pæan !

And of his dread adventures here sing I,
Equivalent with the Punic chivalry,
That brake his lance with terror and renown
Against the gates of slaughtered Remus' town ;

Iö, iö pæan !

And was the first of many thousands more
That at Penichia waded to the shore :
There couth he lead his landed flock so far,
Till 'a was left of men approved in war ;

Iö, iö pæan !

O honour's fire, that not the brackish sea
Mought quench, nor foeman's fearful 'larums lay !
So high those golden flakes don mount and climb
That they exceed the reach of shepherd's rhyme ;

Iö, iö pæan !

PALINODE.

What boot thy welcomes, foolish-hardy swain?
Louder pipes than thine are going on this plain;
Fair Eliza's lasses and her great grooms
Receive this shepherd with unfeigned welcomes.

Honour is in him that doth it bestow;
Thy reed is rough, thy seat is all too low,
To writen sike praise; hadst thou blithe Homer's quill,
Thou moughtst have matter equal with thy skill.

PIERS.

Twit me with boldness, Palin, as thou wilt,
My good mind be my glory and my guilt;
Be my praise less or mickle, all is one,
His high deserts deserven to be known;

Iö, iö pæan!

So cease, my pipe, the worthies to record
Of thilk great shepherd, of thilk fair young lord;
Leave him with luck to those well tunéd lays
That better ken to sound sike shepherd's praise;

Iö, iö pæan!

Now time is near to pen our sheep in fold,
And evening air is rheumatic and cold.
For my late songs plead thou, my pure goodwill!
Though new-come once, brave earl, yet welcome still!

Iö, iö pæan!

THE HONOUR OF THE GARTER. (1593)

See supra p. 7

AD MÆCENATEM PROLOGUS.

PLAIN is my coat, and humble is my gait :
Thrice-noble earl, behold with gentle eyes
My wit's poor worth, even for your noblésse,
Renownéd lord, Northumberland's fair flower,
The Muses' love, patron, and favourite,
That artisans and scholars dost embrace,
And clothest Mathesis in rich ornaments ;
That admirable mathematic skill,
Familiar with the stars and zodiac,
To whom the heaven lies open as her book ;
By whose directions undeceivable,
Leaving our schoolmen's vulgar trodden paths,
And following the ancient reverend steps
Of Trismegistus and Pythagoras,
Through uncouth ways and unaccessible,
Dost pass into the spacious pleasant fields
Of divine science and philosophy ;
From whence beholding the deformities

8 per 100

Of common errors, and world's vanity,
Dost here enjoy that sacred sweet content
That baser souls, not knowing, not affect ;
And so by Fate's and Fortune's good aspéct
Raised, in thy height, and these unhappy times,
Disfurnished wholly of heroical spirits
That learning should with glorious hands uphold,
(For who should learning underbear but he
That knows thereof the precious worthiness,
And sees true science from base vanity ?)
, Hast in regard the true philosophy
That in pure wisdom seats her happiness.
And you the Muses, and the Graces three,
You I invoke from heaven and Helicon,
For other patrons have poor poets none,
But Muses and the Graces, to implore.
Augustus long ago hath left the world,
And liberal Sidney, famous for the love
He bare to learning and to chivalry,
And virtuous Walsingham are fled to heaven.
Why thither speed not Hobbin and his feres,
Great Hobbinol,* on whom our shepherds gaze,

---

* Old edition "Hobbinall."—Hobbinol was the poetic name of Gabriel Harvey, and Colin Clout that of Spenser : but there can be no doubt that Spenser is meant here ; in "England's Helicon," 1600, is a poem attributed to Spenser called "Hobbinol's Dittie in praise of Eliza, Queene of the Shepheards." In our old pastoral every man was, in relation to the duties of his life, a shepherd.

And Harington,* well-lettered and discreet,
That hath so purely naturálizéd
Strange words, and made them all free denizens?
Why thither speeds not Rosamond's trumpeter,†
Sweet as the nightingale? Why go'st not
    thou,
That richly cloth'st conceit with well-made
    words,
Campion, accompanied with | our English
    Fraunce,‡
A peerless sweet translator of our time?
Why follow not a thousand that I know,
Fellows to these, Apollo's favourites,
And leave behind our ordinary grooms,
With trivial humours to pastime the world,
That favours Pan and Phœbus both alike?
Why thither post not all good wits from
    hence,

---

  * Sir John Harington, whose translation of Ariosto's "Orlando Furioso" was first printed in 1591.

  † Samuel Daniel: his "Delia: contayning certaine sonnets;" with "The Complaint of Rosamond," appeared in 1592.

  ‡ Thomas Campion (who was born in 1540 and died in 1623) wrote several poems and masques, which excited no slight contemporary applause. He wrote himself Doctor of Physic, but was, besides poet, a composer of good music, and a writer upon the science of music, and the art of poetry. Abraham Fraunce poured forth English hexameters with great facility. Fraunce, poet and lawyer, published the "Lamentation of Amyntas" in 1587, and "Lawyer's Logic" in 1588.

To Chaucer, Gower, and to the fairest Phaer
That ever ventured on great Virgil's works?
To Watson, worthy many epitaphs
For his sweet poesy, for Amyntas' tears
And joys so well set down?* And after
  thee
Why hie they not, unhappy in thine end,   5 per 100
Marley,† the Muses' darling/for thy verse,
Fit to write passions for the souls below,
If any wretched souls in passion speak?
Why go not all into th' Elysian fields,
And leave this centre barren of repast,
Unless in hope Augusta will restore

---

* The pieces more particularly alluded to here are the following :—
First, "Amyntas Thomæ Watsoni Londinensis J. V. studiosi. Nemini
datur amare simul et sapere. Excudebat Henricus Marsh ex assigna-
tione Thomæ Marsh," 1585, duod., its subject the lamentations of
Amyntas for the death of Phillis. (In the "Phœnix Nest," 1593, is a
copy of verses by Watson, printed also in "England's Helicon," 1600,
entitled "Amintas for his Phillis.") Secondly, "Amintæ Gaudia,
Authore Thoma Watsono Londinensi, juris studioso. Londini,
Impensis Gulihelmi Ponsonbei," 1592, 4to; in the Dedication to
which by C. M. Watson is spoken of as dead. Thomas Watson,
who died at the age of thirty-five, was one of the best Elizabethan
writers of Love Sonnets. He was appreciated by Sir Philip Sidney,
was a friend of Spenser's, and he was himself the Amyntas of his
fellow-poets.

† One of the various ways in which the name of the great dramatist,
Christopher Marlowe, used to be spelt. When he was not quite
thirty years old, he was killed by Francis Archer at Deptford, and
buried there 1st of June, 1593.

The wrongs that learning bears of covetousness,
And court's disdain, the enemy to art?
    Leave, foolish lad, it mendeth not with words;
    Nor herbs nor time such remedy affords.

        Your honour's in all humble service,
                Geo. Peele.

THE HONOUR OF THE HONOURABLE ORDER OF
THE GARTER. *(Ad. 1593)*

About the time when Vesper in the west
Gan set the evening watch, and silent Night,
Richly attended by his twinkling train,
Sent sleep and slumber to possess the world,
And fantasy to hauzen idle heads;
Under the starry canopy of heaven
I laid me down, laden with many cares,
(My bedfellows almost these twenty years,)
Fast by the stream where Thame and Isis meet,
And day by day roll to salute the sea
For more than common service it performed
To Albion's queen, when foemen shipped for
    fight,
To forage England ploughed the ocean up,
And slunk into the channel that divides
The Frenchmen's strand from Britain's fishy
    towns.

Even at that time, all in a fragrant mead,   4 per 100
In sight of that fair castle, that o'erlooks
The forest one way, and the fertile vale
Watered with that renownéd river Thames,
Old Windsor Castle, did I take my rest:
When Cynthia, companion of the Night,
With shining brand lightening his ebon car,
Whose axletree was jet enchased with stars,
And roof with shining ravens' feathers ceiled,
Piercing mine eyelids as I lay along,
Awaked me through.   Therewith methought I
    saw
A royal glimmering light streaming aloft,
As Titan mounted on the Lion's back   3 per 100
Had clothed himself in fiery-pointed beams,
To chase the Night, and entertain the Morn;
Yet scarce had chanticleer rung the midnight
    peal,
Or Phœbe half-way gone her journey through.
Sleeping or waking as alone I lay,
Mine eyes, and ears, and senses all were served
With every object perfect in his kind:
And, lo, a wonder to my senses all!
For through the melting air, perfumed with
    sweets,
I might discern a troop of horsemen ride,
Armed cap-de-pè, with shield and shivering lance;

As in a plash, or calm transparent brook,
We see the glistering fishes scour along ;

5 per 100

A number numberless, appointed well
For tournament, as if the God of War
Had held a jousts in honour of his love,
Or all the sons of Saturn and of Ops
Had been in arms against Enceladus.
Therewith I heard the clarions and the shalms,
The sackbuts, and a thousand instruments
Of several kinds ; and, loudest of them all,
A trump more shrill than Triton's is at sea :

6 per 100

The same Renown, precursor of the train,
Did sound,—for who rings louder than Renown ?
He mounted was upon a flying horse,
And clothed in falcon's feathers to the ground :
By his escutcheon justly might you guess
He was the herald of eternity,
And pursuivant-at-arms to mighty Jove.
I looked to see an end of that I saw,
And still methought the train did multiply ;
And yielding clouds gave way, and men-at-arms
Succeed as fast, one at another's heels,
As in the vast Mediterranean sea
The rolling waves do one beget another.
Those that perfumed the air with myrrh and
    balm,
Dancing and singing sweetly as they went,

Were naked virgins, decked with garlands green,
And seemed the Graces, for with golden chains
They linkèd were, three lovely countenances.
About them Cupid, as to me it seemed,
Lay playing on his parti-coloured wings ;
And sometime on a horse as white as milk
I saw him armed and mounted in the throng,
As Love had right to march with men of war.
Weary of looking up, I laid me down,
Willing to rest, as sleepy souls are wont,
When of a sudden such a noise I heard
Of shot of ordnance pealing in mine ears,
As twenty thousand tire had played at sea,
Or Ætna split had belched her bowels forth,
Or heaven and earth in arms thundering amain
Had bent their great artillery for war,
And weary Atlas had let fall his load ;
Enough to wake Endymion from his trance.
Yet was the welkin clear, nor smoke nor dust
Annoyed mine eyes : I gazed, and, as I looked,
Methought this host of aery armed men
Girt Windsor Castle round. Anon I saw,
Under a canopy of crimson bysse,
Spangled with gold, and set with silver bells
That sweetly chimed and lulled me half asleep,
A goodly king in robes most richly dight,
The upper like a Roman palliament,

Indeed a chaperon, for such it was ;
And, looking nearer, lo, upon his leg
An ancient badge of honour I espied,
A garter brightly glistering in mine eye.
A worthy ornament !   Then I called to mind
What princely Edward, of that name the Third,
King Edward, for his great achievements famed,
What he began,—the Order of Saint George,
That at this day is honoured through the world,
The Order of the Garter so y-clept,
A great effect grown of a slender cause,
Graced by a king, and favoured of his feres,
Famed by his followers, worthy kings and
    queens,
That to this day are sovereigns of the same.
The manner how this matter grew at first
Was thus.   The king, disposéd on a time
To revel, after he had shaken France,
(O, had he bravely held it to the last !)
And decked his lions with their flower-de-lys,
Disposed to revel,—some say otherwise,—
Found on the ground by fortune, as he went,
A lady's garter, and the queen's, I trow,
Lost in a dance, and took it up himself :
It was a silken ribbon weaved of blue.
His lords and standers-by, seeing the king
Stoop for this garter, smiled, as who would say,

"Our office that had been," or somewhat else.
King Edward wistly looking on them all,
With princely hands having that garter seized,
From harmless heart, where honour was engraved,
Bespake in French, ('a could the language well,
And rife was French those days with English-
    men ;
They went to school to put together towns,
And spell in France with fescues made of pikes,)
"Honi soit qui mal y pense," quoth he.
Wherewith upon advisement, though the cause
Were small, his pleasure and his purpose was
T' advance that garter, and to institute
A noble order sacred to Saint George,
And knights to make, whom he would have be
    termed
Knights of the Garter.   This beginning had
This honourable order of our time.
Hereon I thought when I beheld the king ;
But swifter than my thought, by that I saw,
And words I heard or seemed to hear at least,
I was instructed in the circumstance,
And found it was King Edward that did march
In robes like those he ware when with his lords
He held Saint George's royal feast on earth.
His eldest son, surnaméd the Black Prince,—
Though black of hue, that surname yet in France

He wan, for terror to the Frenchmen's hearts,
His countenance was, his sword an iron scourge,—
He on a coal-black courser mounted was,
And in his hand a battle-axe he hent ;
His beaver up ; his corselet was of steel
Varnished as black as jet ; his bases black ;
· And black / from head to foot, yea, horse and
hoof,
As black as night.   But in a twink methought
'A changed at once his habit and his steed,
And had a garter as his father had,
Right rich and costly, with embroidery
Of pearl and gold : I could on it discern
The poesy whereof I spake of yore ;
And well I wot, since this King Edward's days,
Our kings and queens about their royal arms
Have in a garter borne this poesy.
Still as I lay I gazed, and guessed at once
What was this train, and whither it did bend :
I / found at last King Edward was the man,
Accompanied with kings and conquerors,
That from the spacious aery House of Fame
Set forward royally to solemnize
Th' instalment of some new-created knights.
For, lo, I saw in strange accoutrements,
Like to King Edward's and the Prince of Wales',
Full four-and-twenty knights, nor more nor less,

In robes with precious collars of Saint George;
And garters all they had, buckled with gold.
Fame, in a stole of purple set with eyes
And ears and tongues, carried a golden book:
Upon the cover this I saw engraved:

Pauci quos æquus amavit
Iupiter, aut ardens evexit ad æthera virtus,
Dîs geniti.

Methought this saying could not but import
They should be noble men of golden minds
And great account, favoured of prince and peers,
Whose names should in that register be writ,
Consecrate to Saint George's chosen knights.
Herewith the golden book gan open fair,
And earthly I might read their names that next
Went to the king: they were no common men,
For to my seeming each one had a page
That bare a fair escutcheon after him,
Whereon his arms were drawn; I have forgot
Their several coats, but well I wot their names.
And first I saw enrolled within this book
King Edward's name; he was the sovereign.
Their register was Fame. Renown, before
That sounded shrill, was officer-at-arms
And usher to the train; his office-badge
Was a black rod whereof he took his name.
Honour went king-at-arms, next to the knights,

Half-armed, like Pallas shaped for arms and arts,
Rich in habiliments of peace and war :
Ancient and grave he was and sage to see.
Near him went Time, well-pleased and well-content
As if he joyed t' accompany this train,
And in his hand a royal standard bare,
Wherein Saint George was drawn and limned in
    gold.
Under the verge, as title to the book,
Was writ, " Knights of the order of Saint George,
Knights of the Garter."   Edward Prince of Wales
Was first, then Henry Duke of Lancaster,
And Nicholas Earl of Warwick made the third.
Captaine de Buch was next, renowned for arms.
Then the brave Earls of Stafford and Southampton ;
To whose successors, for his sake that lives
And now survives in honour of that name,
To whom my thoughts are humble and devote,
Gentle Wriothesley, Southampton's star,
I wish all fortune, that in Cynthia's eye,
Cynthia the glory of the western world,
With all the stars in her fair firmament,
Bright may he rise and shine immortally.
And Mortimer, a gentle trusty lord,
More loyal than that cruel Mortimer
That plotted Edward's death at Killingworth,
Edward the Second, father to this king,

Whose tragic cry even now methinks I hear,
When graceless wretches murdered him by night.
Then Lisle, and Burwash, Beauchamp, and Mohun,
Grey, Courtney, and the Hollands worthy knights,
Fitz-simon, Wale, and Sir Hugh Wrottesley,
Nele Loryng, Chandos, Sir Miles Stapleton,
Walter Pagannel, Eam, and d'Audley ; last
Was the good knight Sir Sanchet d'Abrichecourt.
These names I read, for they were written fair ;
And, as it seemed to me, these were the first
Created of that order by the king ;
And man by man they marched in equipage.
A many more there were than I could note,
And, sooth to say, I think the book was full ;
And in the train a number infinite,
True knights of all the orders in the world,
Christians and heathens, that accompanied
This worthy king in his procession.
Cæsar himself was there ; I saw him ride,
Triúmphing in his three-and-twenty wounds,
Because they showed the malice of the world.
Pompey was there, the rival of his fame,
That died a death as base and violent.
Leave I this theme : the mightiest that have lived
Have fall'n, and headlong too ; in misery
It is some comfort to have company.
Hector of Troy, and kings ere Troy was built,

Or Thrace was Thrace, were there : old Dardanus,
And Ilus, and Assaracus, came along.
For in the House of Fame what famous man,
What prince, but hath his trophy and his place ?
There Joshua, David, and great Machabee,
Last anchor-hold and stay of Jacob's race,
Did march ; and Macedonian Alexander ;
Victorious Charles the Great, the flower of France ;
Godfrey of Bullen, whom the Christian kings
Created King of great Jerusalem ;
And Arthur, glory of the western world,
And all his knights were in this royal train.
Jason was there, Knight of the Golden Fleece ;
Knights of the Tosson, and of Saint Iago,
Knights of the Rhodes, Knights of the Sepulchre,
Were there : the air was pestered to my thought.
Among them all a worthy man of mark,
A prince of famous memory I saw,
Henry the Eighth, that led a warlike band
Of English earls, and lords, and lusty knights,
That ware the garter sacred to Saint George.
Who was not there ?   I think the court of Fame
Was naked and unpeopled, in this train
There were so many emperors, lords, and kings,
Knights errant and adventurous.   In the book
That on a desk lay open before Fame,
For in a sumptuous chariot did he ride

Of crystal, set with leaves of glittering gold,
And fair tralucent stones, that over all
It did reflect,—within that glorious book
I saw a name rejoicéd me to see,
Francis of Bedford ; I could read it plain,
And glad I was that in that precious book
That name I found, for now methought I said,
Here virtue doth outlive th' arrest of death ;
For dead is Bedford, virtuous and renowned
For arms, for honour, and religious love,
And yet alive his name in Fame's records,
That held this garter dear, and ware it well.
Some worthy wight let blazon his deserts :
Only a tale I thought on by the way,
As I observed his honourable name.
I heard it was his chance, o'erta'en with sleep,
To take a nap near to a farmer's lodge,
Trusted a little with himself belike :
This agéd earl, in his apparel plain,
Wrapt in his russet cloak, lay down to rest,
His badge of honour buckled to his leg,
Bare and unhid.   There came a pilfering swad,
And would have preyed upon this ornament,
And 'sayed t' unbuckle it, thinking him asleep :
The noble gentleman, feeling what he meant,
" Hold, foolish lad," quoth he, " a better prey ;
This garter is not fit for every leg,

And I account it better than my purse."
The varlet ran away ; the earl awaked,
And told his friends, and smiling said withal,
"'A would not, had 'a understood the French
Writ on my garter, dared t' have stoln the same."
This tale I thought upon, told me for truth,
The rather for it praised the poesy,
Right grave and honourable, that importeth much ;
" Ill be to him," it saith, " that evil thinks."
O sacred loyalty, in purest hearts
Thou build'st thy bower ! Thy weeds of spotless
    white,
Like those that stood for Rome's great offices,
Make thee renowned, glorious in innocency.
Why stick I here ? The train cast in a ring
About the castle, making melody,
Under the glorious spreading wings of Fame
I saw a virgin queen, attired in white,
Leading with her a sort of goodly knights,
With garters and with collars of Saint George :
" Elizabeth " on a compartiment
Of gold in bysse was writ, and hung askew
Upon her head, under an imperial crown.
She was the sovereign of the knights she led :
Her face, methought, I knew, as if the same,
The same great empress that we here enjoy,
Had climbed the clouds, and been in person there ;

To whom the earth, the sea, and elements
Auspicious are.   A many that I knew,
Knighted in my remembrance, I beheld,
And all their names were in that register ;
And yet I might perceive some so set down,
That, howsoe'er it hapt I cannot tell,
The carle Oblivion stol'n from Lethe's lake,
Or Envy stept from out the deep Avern,
Had razed, or blemished, or obscured at least.
What have those fiends to do in Fame's fair court ?
Yet in the House of Fame, and courts of kings,
Envy will bite, or snarl and bark at least,
As dogs against the moon that yelp in vain :
Say "*Frustra*" to those curs, and shake thy coat.
And all the kings, since that King Edward's days,
Were with their knights and companies in that train.
When all were whist, King Edward thus bespake :
" Hail, Windsor ! where I sometimes took delight
To hawk, and hunt, and back the proudest horse,
And where in princely pleasure I reposed
In my return from France,"—a little sigh
I heard him fetch withal ; his reason why
I cannot guess ; I think it was for this,
That England had given o'er their traffic there,—
" And twenty times hail, Windsor !" quoth the king,
" Where I have stalled so many hardy knight,
And tournaments and royal justs performed :

Behold, in honour of mine ancient throne,
In honour of fair England, and Saint George,
To whom this Order of the Garter first
I sacred held ; in honour of my knights,
Before this day created and installed,
But specially in honour of those five
That at this day this honour have received
Under Elizabeth, England's great sovereign,—
Northumberland and Worcester, noble earls,
Borough and Sheffield, lords of lively hope,
And honourable old Knowles famed for his sons,
And for his service gracious and renowned ;
Lo, from the House of Fame, with princely trains
Accompanied, and kings, and conquerors,
And knights of proof, loyal and valorous,
I re-salute thee here, and gratulate
To those new knights, created by a queen
Peerless for wisdom and for majesty,
The Honour of the Garter : may they long
Wear them as notes of true nobility
And virtue's ornaments ! Young Northumberland,
Mounted on Fortune's wheel, by virtue's aim
Become thy badge, as it becometh thee,
That Europe's eyes thy worthiness may see.
And, Worcester, what pure honour hath put on
With chaste and spotless hands, in honour wear ;
Answer the noblest of thine ancestry,

In deeds to fame and virtue consecrate.
Borough, brought up in learning and in arms,
Patron of music and of chivalry,
Brandish thy sword in right, and spend thy wits
In commonwealth affairs : it shall become
Thy forwardness to follow virtue's cause,
And great designs of noble consequence.
And, Sheffield, shape thy course no otherwise
Than loyalty, the load-star of renown,
Directs ; that, as thine ancestors have done,
Thine earthly race in honour thou mayst run.
To thee, old man," with kindness quoth the king,
" That reap'st this honour in thy waning age,
See what a trophy Queen Elizabeth
Prepares before thy hearse : long mayst thou live,
And die in fame, that hast well near achieved
The noble Norris' honour in thy sons,
Thrice-noble lord, as happy for his few,
As was the King of Troy for many more."
With that he ceased, and to the foremost earl,—
For why methought I saw them every man,
Stalled in their places and their ornaments,—
" Percy," quoth he, " thou and thy lordly peers,
Your names are in this register of Fame,
Written in leaves and characters of gold :
So live, as with a many more you may
Survive and triumph in eternity,

Out of Oblivion's reach or Envy's shot ;
And that your names immortally may shine
In these recórds, not earthly, but divine."
Then shalms and sackbuts sounded in the air,
But shrill'st of all, the trumpet of Renown ;
And by and by a loud retraite he rung.
The train retired, as swift as stars don shoot,
From whence they came ; and day began to break ;
And with the noise and thunder in the sky,
When Fame's great double-doors fell to and shut,
And this triumphant train was vanished quite,
The gaudy Morn out of her golden sleep
Awaked, and little birds uncaged gan sing
To welcome home the bridegroom of the sea.

EPILOGUS.

Wherewith I roused, recounting what I saw:
And then thought I : were it as once it was,
But long ago, when learning was in price,
And poesy with princes gracious,
I would adventure to set down my dream,
In honour of these new-advancéd lords,
Saint George's knights. I was encouragéd,
And did as I have done ; which humbly here
I yield, as firstlings of my scholar's crop,
Consecrate purely to your noble name,

To gratulate to you this honour's height,
As little boys with flinging up their caps
Congratulate great kings and conquerors.
Take it in gree, fair lord.   " Procul hinc turba
    Invidiosa :
Stirps rudis urtica est, stirps generosa rosa."

                                        G. P.

"BLESSED BE THE HEARTS THAT WISH MY SOVEREIGN WELL."

His golden locks time hath to silver turned ;
  O time too swift, O swiftness never ceasing !
His youth 'gainst time and age hath ever spurned,
  But spurned in vain ; youth waneth by in-
    creasing :
Beauty, strength, youth, are flowers but fading
    seen ;
Duty, faith, love, are roots, and ever green.

His helmet now shall make a hive for bees,
  And, lovers' sonnets turned to holy psalms,
A man-at-arms must now serve on his knees,
  And feed on prayers, which are age his alms :
But though from court to cottage he depart,
His saint is sure of his unspotted heart.

And when he saddest sits in homely cell,
  He'll teach his swains this carol for a song,

"Blessed be the hearts that wish my sovereign
    well,
    Cursed be the souls that think her any wrong!"
Goddess, allow this agéd man his right,
To be your beadsman now that was your knight.

ELIZABETH

BORN, *September* 7, 1533

BECAME QUEEN, *November* 17, 1558

REIGNED 44 *years*, 4 *months and a week*

VICTORIA

BORN, *May* 24, 1819

BECAME QUEEN, *June* 20, 1837

REIGNED 50 *years*

AND ON THE 21ST OF JUNE 1887
SOUGHT THE BLESSING OF GOD
UPON THE CELEBRATION OF HER

GOLDEN WEDDING
TO HER PEOPLE

Grace be with her until the End